Feng Shui

BEFORE & AFTER

Feng Shui

BEFORE & AFTER

STEPHEN SKINNER

Tuttle Publishing
Boston • Rutland, Vermont • Tokyo

First published in the United States in 2001 by Tuttle Publishing, an imprint of Periplus Editions (HK) Ltd,
with editorial offices at 153 Milk Street, Boston, Massachusetts 02109

The text is from Stephen Skinner
The art is from Gareth Williams

ISBN: 0-8048-3283-8

Distributed by:

North America
Tuttle Publishing
Distribution Center
Airport Industrial Park
364 Innovation Drive
North Clarendon
VT 05759-9436
Tel: (802) 773-8930
Tel: (800) 526-2778
Fax: (802) 773-6993

Japan
Tuttle Publishing
RK Building, 2nd Floor
2-13-10 Shimo-Meguro
Meguro-Ku
Tokyo 153 0064
Tel: (03) 5437-0171
Fax: (03) 5437-0755

Asia Pacific
Books Pte Ltd
5 Little Road #08-01
Singapore 536983
Tel: (65) 280-1330
Fax: (65) 280-6290

1 3 5 7 9 10 8 6 4 2
06 05 04 03 02 01 00

A HALDANE MASON BOOK

Editorial Director: Sydney Francis
Art Director: Ron Samuel
Editors: Beck Ward, Andrew Duncan
Design & computer graphics: Phil Ford, Zoë Mellors
Artwork: Gareth Williams
Picture research: Sorrel Everton
Index: Lydia Darbyshire

Printed in Hong Kong

Picture acknowledgements

Cover photography by Sydney Francis, Elizabeth Whiting & Associates, the Garden Picture Library/
John Glover and *Feng Shui For Modern Living*
All photography by Elizabeth Whiting & Associates with the exception of the following: **Oxford Scientific Film:** /Larry Crowhurst 2–3;
Feng Shui For Modern Living: 7, 14, 22, 34 (centre top, centre, centre bottom), 42 (top), 43 (top), 51 (top), 55 (bottom), 58, 82
(bottom), 84 (top); **Sydney Francis:** 9, 10 (centre top, centre, centre bottom, bottom), 18 (centre left, centre, centre right, right), 19 (top
centre, top right, centre right, bottom right), 37 (centre top, centre, centre bottom, bottom), 90 (centre left); **Shandwick Welbeck:** 16
(both); **Graham Price:** 17 (top); **Robert Harding Picture Library:** 10 (top), 18 (far left), 37 (top), 90 (centre right); **Garden Picture
Library:** /J.S. Sira 25, /Eric Crichton 83, /Howard Rice 84 (bottom); **Image Bank:** /Gary Russ 46

Title pages: *Water is fundamental to feng shui, and is one of the main vehicles
for both harboring and conducting ch'i, the energy at the heart of feng shui.*

Contents

Introduction

HOW TO USE THIS BOOK

This book is designed so that you can use it even if you have never read anything else about feng shui. Obviously you will have to adapt the general makeover advice to the specific situation and condition of your own home, office, or garden.

First read the background chapters on feng shui to orient yourself. Then start thinking through what really needs changing in your life. While in this frame of mind, read through the room descriptions, studying the before and after illustrations for practical hints and tips.

When you are ready to start planning your own feng shui changes, use some graph paper and clear acetate, or tracing paper, (available from most good craft stores) to help you.

Draw an accurate plan of the space you wish to change onto a piece of the graph paper, marking on it the position of North. Next, take the acetate, or tracing paper, and, using a fine marker, draw the pa kua (see page 22) onto one piece and the lo shu square (see page 26) on to another. Lay either of these over the top of your plan, lining up North, to see which changes you need to make in each of the different sectors.

After this comes the exciting part—implementing your feng shui changes!

The point of any makeover is to change, with the aim of improving, your home, office, or garden. The point of this book is to give your makeovers that extra edge; don't just be satisfied with changing your interior environment—make this change also work for you. The best definition I have ever heard of feng shui is "luck engineering." To the western mind, however, this sounds like a crazy idea—how can you engineer your luck?

Well, think about it a bit. We probably all know friends who have fantastic homes, along with great jobs, for whom opportunities seem to drop like ripe fruit into their hands. We also have friends who live in dull, cramped, cluttered environments, for whom life is always a struggle, who move back two paces for each pace they move forward. Their homes seem to be as congested as their luck. Maybe we even envy the first couple, and feel some compassion for the second.

The question is, which came first? Did the luck of such people enable them to afford a great home to live in, with beautiful furnishings; or did the advantages of a bright and positive environment enable them to reach that little bit further to seize opportunities that might otherwise have passed them by?

Feng shui says that opportunities come when the environment is right. Hence, feng shui is the art and science of making the environment so supportive that your attitude, opportunities, and luck change for the better.

Feng shui was completely unheard of back in 1976, when I wrote the first book published on this subject in England. In the 1990s feng shui expert Lillian Too began to popularize it with her own books and advice. Since then, feng shui has become commonplace to the point that almost anyone you ask will recognize it. Many of us, however, are starting to acknowledge that lives rooted in the warm environment of a good home will grow and expand, and so instinctively they can more easily understand the basis of feng shui.

Feng shui is an art, just like interior decoration, in that it takes judgment and experience to get right. It is, however, also a science, as its more recondite depths require quite complex calculations. We will, however, not be examining these in this book.

It is important to understand that feng shui is not just intuition. You cannot "do" feng shui simply by feel. There are rules and they need to be adhered to or it will not work.

You will find that feng shui makeovers require a bit more than just a few cans of paint and some rolls of wallpaper. Feng shui requires an eye—one that sees how a living space relates to others, and one that spots alignments never noticed before. Feng shui changes require the use of elements like water (have you installed a fish tank or an indoor fountain recently?,) earth (now might be the time to buy some of those beautiful quartz crystals), metal (so that's where the filing cabinets go), and wood (indoor plants are certainly part of the dynamics of feng shui).

Feng shui needs for you to evaluate your life and what you want out of it. By the time you have absorbed the basic rules, you will find yourself spotting the glaring feng shui mistakes in other people's living spaces. Suddenly, so much of what you feel instinctively will become clear—feng shui will provide the reasons for those reactions and make sense of the instincts you already have. More importantly, it gives you the necessary tools to do something about your life if you feel listless or stuck.

Do not underestimate its power. What the Chinese have spent millennia perfecting, we now have instant access to. Feng shui ranks alongside acupuncture, kung fu, even gunpowder as an art or science that the Chinese have, almost reluctantly, finally revealed to the West. Use it and prosper.

Above: *The curved path, water feature, metal bench, and plants in this back garden are all excellent feng shui.*

Below: *Feng shui can benefit any part of your house, including a small home office or study.*

Above: *Ch'i, the stuff of feng shui, an energy subtle, yet pervasive.*

You might ask: does feng shui work, and how can you prove it? Even science "proves" things only by repeating the same procedure many times and getting the same result. Similarly, you can repeat the procedures of feng shui many times and get the same results, as many feng shui masters will attest. The best test, of course, is to use feng shui and see what happens—I am sure you will be pleasantly surprised.

There are examples of rich clients who pay out large fees year after year for effective feng shui advice, but there are also steps you can take yourself that don't involve an expensive feng shui master to work out. With a little application and practice you can do your own feng shui.

Pronunciation and meaning

Among of the first things anybody asks about feng shui is how do you pronounce it and what does it mean. The usual response is that it is pronounced "foong schway." But of course that is not entirely true, as different dialects across China result in varying pronunciations, such as "fun soo-ee" and, in Thailand, "hong soo-ee." There is no English word that translates the concept, so we have to stick with the Chinese.

What does "feng shui" mean? Well, literally it means "wind and water," but this is more of a translation than an explanation. Feng shui relies on the movement of invisible energy, or, as the Chinese call it, ch'i, as carried by the wind and water.

Below: *The lung, or Chinese dragon, is a creature of water and air, not a fire-breathing, cave-dwelling western dragon. Ch'i is sometimes called the dragon's breath, and its manifestation can sometimes be seen in the movement of mist at dawn.*

Ch'i energy

To understand feng shui, you have to accept the idea of ch'i—invisible energy. This should not be too difficult for anyone living in the 21st century, as we have all grown up with the knowledge that among the physical things of this world lie a welter of hidden energies—radio waves, X-rays, microwaves, TV satellite transmissions, infrared rays—and most of these have been discovered only in the last 100 years. Most of us accept these quite readily and, because we can see the devices that supposedly use or create them, we never doubt their existence.

There are, however, other natural energies which have not yet been noticed by western science. Feng shui works with one of those energies—ch'i. This energy flows through the earth and the air, just as surely as radio waves "flow" through the air. Ch'i energy is like the energy brought to bear by a kung fu master when he uses his hands to break bricks which the rest of us would have trouble cracking with a hammer.

Ch'i is a source of prosperity, harmony, health and honor. To be of most benefit, it must be allowed to accumulate gently. But it must never be trapped, otherwise it will stagnate and turn into bad ch'i, which brings ill luck.

Ch'i is strongly affected by bodies of water such as rivers and lakes. These can help accumulate ch'i, but they must be the right type of water. Rivers, for example, should be slow and meandering: too fast flowing and they will carry all the ch'i away.

Above: *The Chinese characters for feng, meaning air or wind (top), and shui, meaning water (bottom).*

Below: *Water, especially in river form, is at the heart of feng shui.*

1

Principles of Feng Shui

Ch'i is energy. Where this energy is absent, life is barren and unproductive. Where ch'i gathers, life is rich and full of opportunities and the people living there are "luckier." This book is all about achieving home, office, and garden makeovers to introduce more ch'i into your life and thus move you up toward the "luckier" end of the spectrum.

The three basic concepts behind feng shui are Alignment, Direction, and Location. More trouble and misunderstanding have been caused by misinterpretation of these apparently simple terms than by any of the complex calculations of a feng shui master, so it is important to be aware of their true meaning.

Alignment

Ch'i needs to accumulate in order to be beneficial. If it moves along straight lines, it gathers speed and becomes destructive. Such fast-flowing ch'i is called sha ch'i. If there are long straight stretches of road, this sha ch'i increases in speed and is destructive when it reaches the end of this alignment.

This is why it is traditionally said that houses at the end of the long leg of a T junction have bad feng shui. It has been noted that houses in this position often change hands frequently, and that a business in such a location will have a much higher chance of going bust. Ideally, you need to be located where the ch'i meanders, in the inner bend of a river or road. These observations have led to the development of various rules for both the inside and outside of buildings. Here we will be most interested in the interior impact of these rules in the home or office. Long corridors so beloved of 1960s planners, are classic cases of a feng shui no-no. Likewise, desks placed in long, straight rows are not conducive to good office feng shui. In homes, through halls need to be broken up by the introduction of strategically placed plants or wind chimes. Doors that are directly opposite each other need also to be separated by wind chimes. Three doors in a row are considered particularly bad.

Any long, straight alignment must be avoided because the "poison arrows" so formed hit whatever is located at the end and damage its feng shui. In 19th-century China, long, straight stretches of railroad tracks were hated for their bad feng shui features. One line from Shanghai was even bought by local Chinese businessmen so that they could destroy it.

When you are doing a makeover, watch out for such alignments. Because much furniture is square or rectangular, alignments pointing at something are almost inevitable. What you need to avoid is sitting directly in the line of these alignments.

Curves should be introduced not just for aesthetic reasons, but also to allow the ch'i to circulate freely. Some feng shui practitioners who feel they can perceive the flow of ch'i portray it as circulating slowly through a room in wide curves, gently collecting but never stagnating.

Below: *The table, pictures, and door all conspire to form an alignment that introduces ch'i too rapidly into the home.*

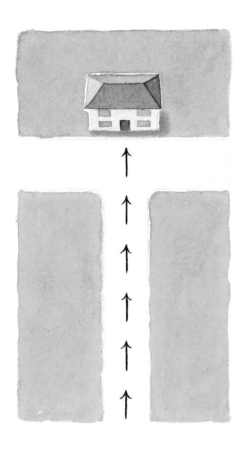

A house situated at the end of a T junction (left) not only has the chance of a wayward car crashing into its front but is also subjected to a constant assault from the fast-moving energy brought to its door by traffic.

Living in a house situated on a curve or bend in the road (right) allows the pace of the ch'i to slow, as well as of the cars themselves.

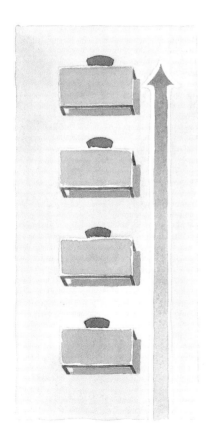

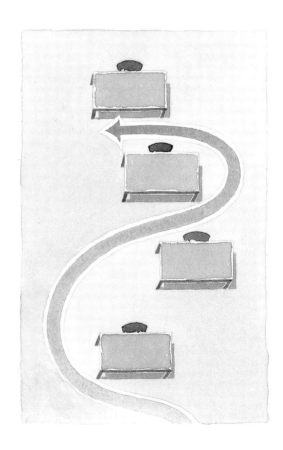

Old-fashioned, rigid office layouts (left) encourage beneficial ch'i to rush past and also create "poison arrows" which are particularly damaging to any desk at the end of the arrow.

A change to the staggered desks (right) forces beneficial ch'i to meander and therefore slow down.

Direction & Location

One of the main tools of the feng shui practitioner is the lo p'an or feng shui compass. In feng shui, Directions are key. There are four cardinal compass points; North (N), South (S), East (E) and West (W). Between them are four inter-cardinal points: Northwest (NW), Northeast (NE), Southwest (SW) and Southeast (SE). These eight Directions correspond to the eight Trigrams of Chinese metaphysics (see page 22). Each of these in turn is divided into three subsections, making a total of 24 Directions, which is the number usually shown on Chinese maritime compasses.

Here, however, we deal only with the familiar eight Directions. Feng shui conventions always show South at the top of the page. This does not alter the fact that South is South; the only difference is the way the compass is drawn on paper.

Basically, if you are standing anywhere in your home, office, or garden, these eight Directions are the eight possible Directions you can turn and face from where you are standing. It is of no account if you sit temporarily at a particular table in a restaurant or on a chair in a friend's house that does not face in an auspicious Direction for you. The things that count are those Directions that you face for long periods of time—like your sleeping or working position—plus orientations that occur at critical times, such as a job interview, signing a key contract or getting married. For these, it is worth checking the time and the Direction.

Remember also that anywhere you spend long periods of time is important from a feng shui perspective, because these places imprint us with their influence. The bedroom, for example, is one of the key rooms for feng shui, because we spend about a third of our lives there.

Science accepts that at a cellular level the body certainly responds to the Direction in which it sleeps. The mitrochondria—those tiny magnetic parts of the cell that provide the cell with its energy—will actually line up if the body is lying on a magnetic North to South alignment. If the body is lying in another Direction, the mitrochondria will take up apparently random positions. Do not confuse Direction with Location. Location refers to the parts of a building, whereas Direction refers to the way you should orient people within the building.

Below: *A full-scale professional San He lo p'an or feng shui compass is used to determine the quality of ch'i flowing through any particular site, home, or office.*

For example, given a free hand by the architect to allocate different rooms in a new house, you might locate the master bedroom toward the rear of the house, away from the over-energetic main entrance. You might avoid locating one of the "wet" rooms, such as the bathroom, in a good Location. It is preferable to place these rooms in unfavorable locations where they will satisfactorily press down on bad luck.

Location is used to determine the different types of feng shui energies in the different parts of the office, home or garden. You need to place a "tic-tac-toe"-type grid over a floor plan to divide the space up into nine approximately equal areas. Thus you can plot—for example, the Northwest corner of a building or garden to determine what feng shui influences are at work there. The area you have marked off is the Northwest Location. This is not the same as standing in the Southern section and facing in a Northwest Direction. Make sure you understand the difference between facing a Northwest Direction and being in a Northwest Location.

Locations are used for diagnosing the feng shui influences in a particular fixed part of the home, office or garden, but Directions are used in relation to the facing Direction of people—that is which way they should sit or sleep. It's a bit confusing initially, but simple once you have this distinction clearly in your head.

On the other hand, Direction consists of placing the human occupants of the room facing their best Directions—see pages 30—31. Everyone has four good Directions and four inauspicious Directions which are personal to the individual concerned. Seats they use regularly should be pointed in one of their best Directions.

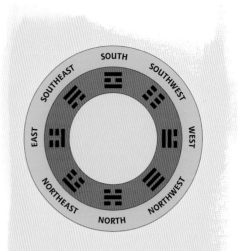

The eight Trigrams, or pa kua, arranged in the so-called Earlier Heaven Sequence. This is used to characterize the type of energy found in the corresponding eight parts of a building.

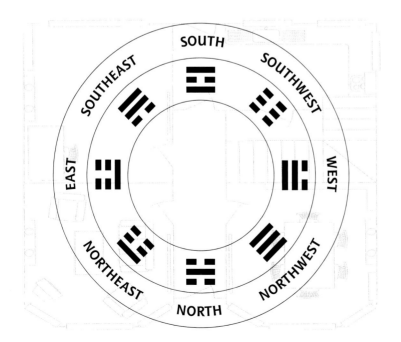

Left: *The eight Trigrams are aligned with the floor plan of your house and indicate the type of energy prevalent in each Location. For example, the room in the bottom right is affected predominantly by the ch'ien Trigram (made up of three solid lines). This is the archetypal male and paternal Trigram. At the simplest level, this might indicate a room suitable for the male head of the house. At a deeper level, ch'ien corresponds to mentors and networking, and the Element Metal. It might, therefore, be a good room in which to locate a home office.*

Yin & yang

YIN COLORS

YANG COLORS

Above: *Yin colors tend to be at the blue end of the spectrum, and include all muddy, bruised, and dark colors. Yang colors tend to be up at the red end of the spectrum and are especially the light, bright colors.*

Left: *Ch'ien is the archetypal male and paternal Trigram, the three unbroken lines portraying a strong yang.*

Left: *K'un is the Mother, the eternal female, made up of three broken, penetrated, or female lines. No Trigram is more yin.*

Chinese science starts not with the "big bang" theory, but with the division of the Great Absolute into yin and yang. Both this and the Western way of looking at the beginning of the Universe are equally symbolic representations of what really occurred, which is beyond human comprehension.

The Chinese division of everything into either yin or yang has an immediate practical use that no amount of ingenuity can give to the Western physicists' "big bang." For the Chinese, "yang" is a word that includes everything overt, bright, active, and masculine; while "yin" conveys the secret, dark, passive, feminine side of the universe. This concept can be applied to almost everything: day and night, bright and dark, active and passive, masculine and feminine.

If you think about these pairs, you can see that they can be applied equally to the decoration of the home, the preparation of food, or the delineation of moods. When we speak of a room needing to be yang, it is immediately obvious that it needs to be decorated and furnished using hot, positive colors, such as reds, yellows, and oranges. In a yin room such as a bedroom, cool, passive colors like blue are needed.

Chinese metaphysics continues by showing that all the things that make up our existence consist of different combinations of yin and yang, just as all the colors known to man are made up of the combination of primary yin or yang colors.

As we know, feng shui is all about balance, so getting the balance of yin and yang right is a large part of the practice of feng shui. The dynamic balance of yin and yang encourages the effective flow of ch'i—the subtle "nutrient" that affects our lives. It is this ch'i that is manipulated by effective feng shui, by the correct interior decoration, and this manipulation is facilitated by an understanding of yin and yang.

Yin is symbolized by –– or the broken line, while yang is symbolized by —— or the unbroken line. These broken and unbroken lines are combined to make the building blocks of feng shui, the eight Trigrams which we will meet on page 22.

Rooms are often obviously yin or yang for various reasons. Strong colors, not mixed, tend to be yang, especially those

toward the red end of the spectrum. Yin colors are usually darker, more mixed, and closer to the blue end of the spectrum. Womb-like rooms tend to be yin, while well-lit and ventilated rooms are yang. Rooms containing striking features tend to be yang, while rooms that say "ignore me please" are yin.

The Tai Ch'i symbol—the symbol that looks like two interlocked tadpoles, one black (yin) and one white (yang)—gives away a little decorating secret. If you look closely, you can see that each contains a little fleck of its opposite—i.e., the yin tadpole contains a yang spot, and vice versa. The trick to energize a yang area is to charge it with a little yin spot. To wake up a yin area, charge it with a little yang color.

A practical example is to use a spot for red (yang Fire) to stimulate the otherwise yin-looking yellow of Earth. Such a combination does very well in the Southwest, where Romance and Marriage are stimulated, or in the Northeast, where the opposite quality of studying is stimulated by a similar color combination.

Above and below: *Rooms that make bold statements in color and design tend to be yang, while rooms decorated in cool, passive colors tend to be yin.*

The five Elements

Another key to manipulating the ch'i in the home, office or garden is the five so-called Elements: Earth, Fire, Water, Wood, and Metal. It is easy to confuse them with the four elements of the Ancient Greek philosophers: Earth, Fire, Water, and Air. Rather than the literal earth or water, which immediately springs to mind from reading their names, however, the Chinese Elements are more correctly thought of as changing energies with five different sets of qualities.

The meaning of the five Elements is thus a lot more complex. Wood, for example, includes both the dead timber that carpenters use (yin Wood) and live plants that exemplify the essence of growth—a much more positive, or yang, attribution. The force that propels the first shoots of spring through the hard soil is closer to the Element Wood than the dead material that a table, for example, is made from. Likewise, Metal stands not just for all metals but man-made, fabricated things and the wealth that flows from them. Metal also means gold, which is the essence of stored prosperity. Earth includes the crystals and gems found in the earth. Water has a very special property, that of being able to carry ch'i—its special place in feng shui is acknowledged by its being the only Element to appear in the term feng shui (shui means water). In fact the Chinese for Element, hsing, has often been translated as "moving agent."

Water is the embodiment of flow, and it acts both to carry ch'i and as a boundary to ch'i. This is part of the reason why the inner

Below: *Each Element has a Primary Direction where it "lives." It also has a Secondary Direction where it helps produce another Element (see page 20), for which this is a Primary Direction.*

Elements and Directions

Element	Fire	Water	Earth	Wood	Metal
Primary Direction	South	North	Center	East	West
Secondary Direction	SW, NE	SE, East	West, NW	South	North

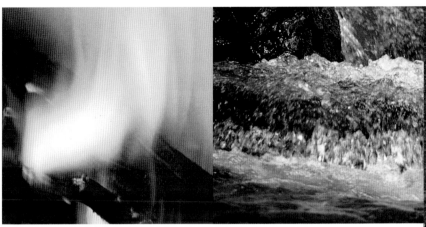

bend of a river is a good place to build—it acts like a purse in capturing beneficial ch'i.

Although the Elements are symbolized by fire, rushing water, rocks, plants, and gold coins, they are much more. Everything in the manifest Universe can be categorized as one or other of these Elements.

- **Fire** is very much a moving agent in its ability to change or transmute other things.
- **Water** is anything that flows, which has a mystical affinity with wealth.
- **Wood** is all growing vegetative life, not just dead timber but also sprouting grass seed.
- **Earth** is the soil from which all vegetative life springs, not Earth in the sense of the third planet from the Sun.
- **Metal** includes not just mineral wealth but also man-made objects fashioned from metal.

The five Elements help to sum up anything that is associated with them. They also form an easy way to identify the correct elements of your feng shui makeover, where the most important associations are, and how the five Elements relate to the eight compass Directions.

The attribution looks a bit asymmetrical, and the ambiguous position of Earth at the Center negotiates the apparent difficulty of attributing five Elements to four main Directions. To find the correct positioning for each of the five Elements in your overall interior design, you will need a compass. Set it down in the center of each room, align the red part of the needle with North, and you will be able to identify each of the eight main compass Directions.

Above: *The Elements are often used to portray the natural world, but to the Chinese they are much more: they signify the principles and phases, as well as the building blocks, of creation.*

The cycle

of the five Elements

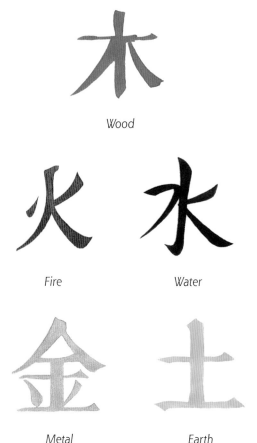

Wood

Fire   Water

Metal   Earth

Above: *The Chinese characters for the five Elements are elegant in their simplicity and carry with them some of the quality of that Element.*

The five Elements continually produce and destroy each other's energies in a special sequence. This sequence is the key to concentrating them, or enhancing them, so that the correct feng shui results occur. If this is starting to sound technical, don't worry—it's quite straightforward, but important to be aware of; a correct understanding of these five Elements is perhaps the most useful of all the things you can learn about feng shui.

The five Elements relate to each other in a number of different ways. The two most commonly known are the Production and Destruction Cycles. These Cycles are a convenient and important guide to the effect various changes in Element concentration can have on the feng shui of a home, office or garden.

The Production Cycle

The purpose of the Production Cycle of the Elements is to find out which Element helps another Element to grow. Water helps Wood to grow. Wood feeds Fire, which produces Earth (ash), out of which springs veins of Metal, from which comes Water.

If you are doing a feng shui makeover of a room and you want to increase the amount of Wood Element, using this cycle you could, for example, build in Water features like aquariums or fountains in the appropriate part of the room, because Water feeds Wood.

The Destruction Cycle

This operates in the reverse direction and is used if you need to reduce the impact of an Element in a room. The cycle is as follows: Water destroys Fire, which melts Metal, which cuts down Wood, which draws energy from the Earth, which, in turn, clogs up and muddies Water. So, if a room is perhaps painted entirely red and is, therefore, heavily Fire energized, you could repaint it. Or instead, to achieve a much more rapid effect, you could destroy some of that Fire by adding a Water feature.

So here we have shown how a Water feature can either enhance the Wood energies in a room or reduce the impact of Fire energies, using the two different Cycles of the five Elements as our guide.

Another cycle, which relates the five Elements together, is the seasonal cycle through the year. To the South is the warmth and yang of the summer sun, the Element Fire. To the North is the yin cold and wet Water of winter. To the East is Wood, which expresses the vegetative growth of spring. Its opposite is the of the West, the setting sun, and the harvesting and scything of the crops with Metal tools. In the Center, Earth holds the balance of the other Elements.

In the Northern hemisphere, where feng shui was discovered, the Elements fit perfectly with the cycle of the seasons, the cycle of growth, death and rebirth. There is considerable controversy as to how the Trigrams and Elements should be applied in the Southern hemisphere. The traditionalist view is that they should be treated exactly the same as in the Northern hemisphere. This unfortunately divorces them from the procession of seasons, which are reversed in the Southern hemisphere. Feng shui experts are still divided on this issue.

Some more clues as to the qualities of the Elements can be derived from their characters. The Chinese characters for three of the five Elements are remarkably similar, and essentially simple. The character for Wood resembles a tree. The primitive character for Water looked somewhat like a meandering stream, but this is not preserved in the modern character. Fire has a similar rhythm about its brushstrokes. The character for Earth has a remarkable solidity and has been likened to the layers of soil, with a plant pushing through into the light. The most complex is Metal, which incidentally also means gold. This character suggests the character for Earth, surmounted by a house roof, implying that Metal, the fruit of the earth, has been taken indoors, for human use.

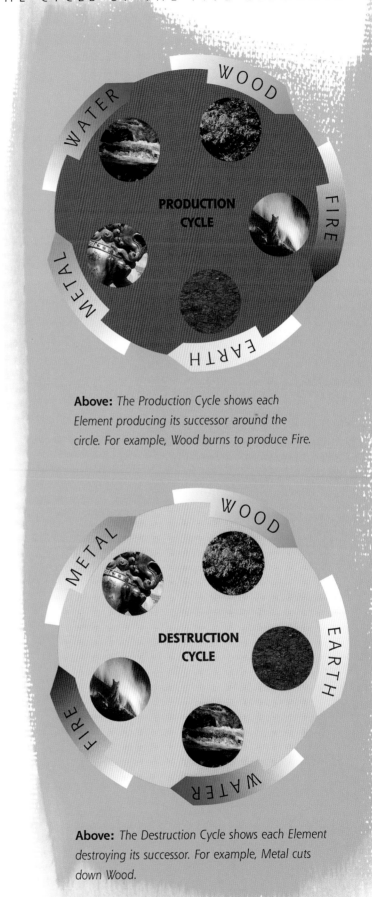

Above: *The Production Cycle shows each Element producing its successor around the circle. For example, Wood burns to produce Fire.*

Above: *The Destruction Cycle shows each Element destroying its successor. For example, Metal cuts down Wood.*

The eight Trigrams
or pa kua

Above: *The Trigrams, arranged in the Earlier Heaven Sequence and mounted on an octagonally framed mirror, form one of the most famous tools of feng shui, the pa kua mirror, which is designed to reflect back to its source any "poison arrow" aimed at a building. Pa kua mirrors are most often seen mounted above windows and doors at the end of T junctions. They are designed for exterior use; do not use them inside.*

A Trigram is a set of three yin (broken) or yang (unbroken) lines (see page 16). There are precisely eight different ways you can combine three yin or yang lines, and therefore there are eight Trigrams. In Chinese "eight Trigrams" translates as pa (eight) kua (Trigrams) or, if you prefer the modern pinyin way of writing it, bagua.

Although pa kua literally means eight Trigrams, the phrase has come to refer to a specific eight-sided figure with the eight Trigrams arranged around its edge. These Trigrams can be arranged in a total of 8 x 8 = 64 different ways, but there are two arrangements that are particularly well known: the oldest layout is the Earlier Heaven Sequence, which is how the Trigrams are seen on most of the octagonal mirrors so beloved by feng shui practitioners. The second arrangement is the Later Heaven Sequence, used to map the internal feng shui layout of the home or office.

The table opposite ties together the eight Trigrams, eight Directions, five Elements and the seasons. Each of the eight Directions has a different life interest or "Aspiration" attributed to it. Instead of simply looking at them circularly in turn, it makes them easier to remember if you consider them in pairs.

Right: *The Trigrams here are arranged in the Later Heaven Sequence and are used indoors, in this case, to locate the Elements and Trigrams in the rooms of a house.*

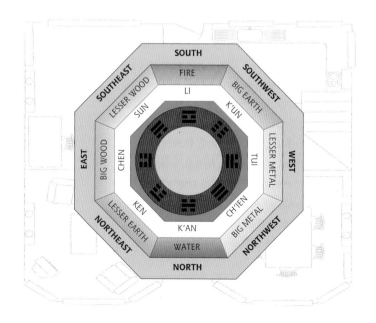

Trigams with associated Elements, Directions, Emblems, Seasons & Life Aspirations

Trigram		Element	Direction	Emblem	Associated Season	Life Aspiration
	Ch'ien	Metal	NW	Heaven	Late Autumn	Mentors & Networking
	K'un	Earth	SW	Earth	Late Summer Early Autumn	Romance & Marriage
	Chen	Wood	E	Thunder	Spring	Family & Ancestors
	K'an	Water	N	Moon & Water	Midwinter	Career
	Ken	Lesser Earth	NE	Mountain	Early Spring	Education & Knowledge
	Sun	Lesser Wood	SE	Wind	Early Summer	Prosperity & Wealth
	Li	Fire	S	Sun & Lightning	Summer	Fame & Recognition
	Tui	Lesser Metal	W	Lake & Seawater	Mid-autumn	Children

The East is seen as being associated with your ancestors and your family in general. The opposite direction on the pa kua is West, and it is associated with your descendants or, more specifically, your children. North and South are also connected: North relates to your career, while South relates to fame, or the respect you receive from your peers. A less obvious pair are Northwest and its opposite, Southeast. Northwest is associated with mentors or networking, while Southeast is the wealth and prosperity created by such networking. Finally Northeast correlates with education and exam success, while Southwest is concerned with romance and a successful marriage.

The pa kua shows the Trigrams and associated Directions and Aspirations. The theory is that different types of ch'i arrive from and/or accumulate in different parts of the room or house. These attributions are important in using the "Eight House" analysis of a room or building. By knowing what part of a house or room to energize, you can decide how and where to make feng shui changes.

OTHER TRADITIONS

The Black Hat Sect school of feng shui, founded in 1986, places the li Trigram farthest from the main door, regardless of compass directions.

Certain practitioners in the Southern hemisphere think it necessary to invert the pa kua and place the li Trigram in the North. We will stick with the traditional feng shui usage in this book. Traditional Compass feng shui places them with the li Trigram always on the southern edge of the pa kua.

Celestial Animals

Below: *The ideal site for a house is in an area protected from strong wings by crescent-shaped hills and fronted by a curving stream. The rear of the house is protected by the Black Tortoise hill, which offers support. Looking out from the house, the lower hill to the right is usually referred to as the White Tiger, while the slightly higher (more yang) hill to the left is the Azure Dragon. In front, the low rise is referred to as the Red Phoenix, or Bird.*

Feng shui was originally concerned with the relationship between buildings and their surrounding landscape. The ideal positioning of a building was explained in terms of what land-form feature was particularly desirable in each of the four Directions, as you look out from the structure. The most important feature was considered to be a high mountain behind the building, symbolized by the Black Tortoise or Turtle. In front of the site it was thought that there should be running water, like a stream or river, and a low rise, called the Red Phoenix.

Looking away from the house from the front door, the left side was meant to have a low range of encircling hills—the Azure

Dragon—with an even lower range to the right—the White Tiger. Feng shui is strong on symbolism, and this is one of the key sets of symbols. Although traditionally the building is thought of as facing South, every building has these four Animals in exactly the same position with regard to the front door of the building, irrespective of the direction in which the building happens to face.

Using the colors associated with the four Celestial Animals in decorating is very important. The table on this page shows which Direction is associated with which color, in turn reflecting the five Elements.

The Celestial Animals are most useful when checking the feng shui of the surrounding garden. Here they can help, for example, to site a rock garden, which might replicate the symbolic Black Tortoise mountain and support the back of the house. Obviously it would not be good feng shui to place this at the front or even the sides of a home or office. Likewise, if there were some doubt as to what color to apply to a wall on the left-hand side of the house (as you are looking out), then you need only verify that it is in the position of the Azure/Green Dragon to pick the most appropriate color to use.

It may seem strange that the Tiger is selected as a yin image. But remember that it is the rare White Tiger of the snowy ranges of western China, and that culturally white is considered the color of death, the ultimate yin. The Dragon, on the other hand, is the azure of the seas of Eastern China, also the green of spring, and of yang growth.

Bearing this in mind, it is important not to over emphasize the White Tiger, at least not inside the house. In fact, in houses where the exterior right-hand side is stronger than the left-hand side (looking out from the front door) you should endeavor to reverse this configuration. The neighboring house may be higher on that side, or the Dragon side might be missing altogether. For example, the left-hand end (looking out) of a row of houses will always have a weakened Dragon side and will suffer from too much yin. The woman of the house is often much stronger than the male in houses in this position.

A weak Dragon side can be partially rectified by, for example, strengthening it with strong yang lighting or, conversely, by diminishing the opposite Tiger side by hiding or painting it in such a way that it loses its dominance. The observance of the four Celestial Animals is primarily concerned with the surrounding influences, rather than the interior of the house.

The four Celestial Animals

Animal	Direction	Color	Element
Black Turtle	North	Black	Water
Azure Dragon	East	Azure/Green	Wood
Red Phoenix	South	Red	Fire
White Tiger	West	White/Metallic	Metal
	Center	Yellow	Earth

Above: *A rock garden, symbolizing the Black Tortoise mountain, can provide support to the back of a house.*

The lo shu

magic square

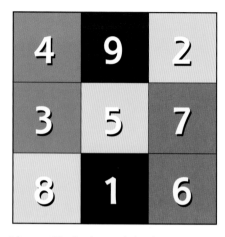

Above: *The basic magic lo shu square, whose numbers always add to 15, no matter in which direction you add them.*

Below: *Tracing the numbers of the lo shu square in their correct numerical sequence produces the pattern in which the Flying Stars move through the lo shu.*

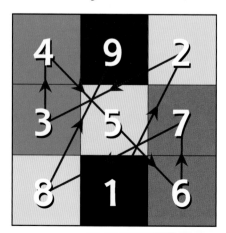

The lo shu square is a three by three "magic" square which contains the numbers one through nine in such a way that whichever way you add up the columns, rows or diagonals, you always arrive at 15. Tradition says that this square dates back to about 2205 B.C.

Take the square and superimpose it on a floor plan of your house. The square containing nine, the strongest yang number, should be located on the South side of your home, while the square containing the number one, also a yang number, should fit with the Northern side. If your home has its main walls pointing to the cardinal points of the compass (North, South, East, West), then it will fit nicely over the floor plan. If, on the other hand, the corners point to the cardinal points of the compass, then the lo shu is placed on it in a diagonal fashion, so that nine still coincides with South.

The colors used in the nine cells of the lo shu offer you a very restricted palette, but a little ingenuity in furnishing and decorating can help to introduce the signature of the Element in the appropriate sector of the building. So that while you might not paint the walls of the room located in the South of your home in a bright red, you can introduce the Element of Fire by the selective use of red, perhaps in a featured picture, or in hangings against a more neutral background wall color.

If you trace your fingers over the square, starting with the box containing the number one and ending up at nine, you will have traced a pattern that is used in advanced Flying Star feng shui. As the numbers move from square to square, so the "eras"—groups of 3 x 20 years—the years, and the months change. This is the basis of "time dimension" feng shui for, as we all know, luck changes with the passing of time. The present luck period lasts from 1984 to 2003, with a new period beginning in 2004.

Flying Star feng shui is beyond the scope of this book. Just bear in mind that it is a more sophisticated use of the lo shu than merely using it to locate the five Elements in the nine different parts of the building or room.

Right: *How the lo shu square looks when placed over the floor plan of a building. In this case, a small lean-to addition is ignored. Typically, diagrams in most feng shui books show the lo shu neatly fitting a house perfectly oriented.*

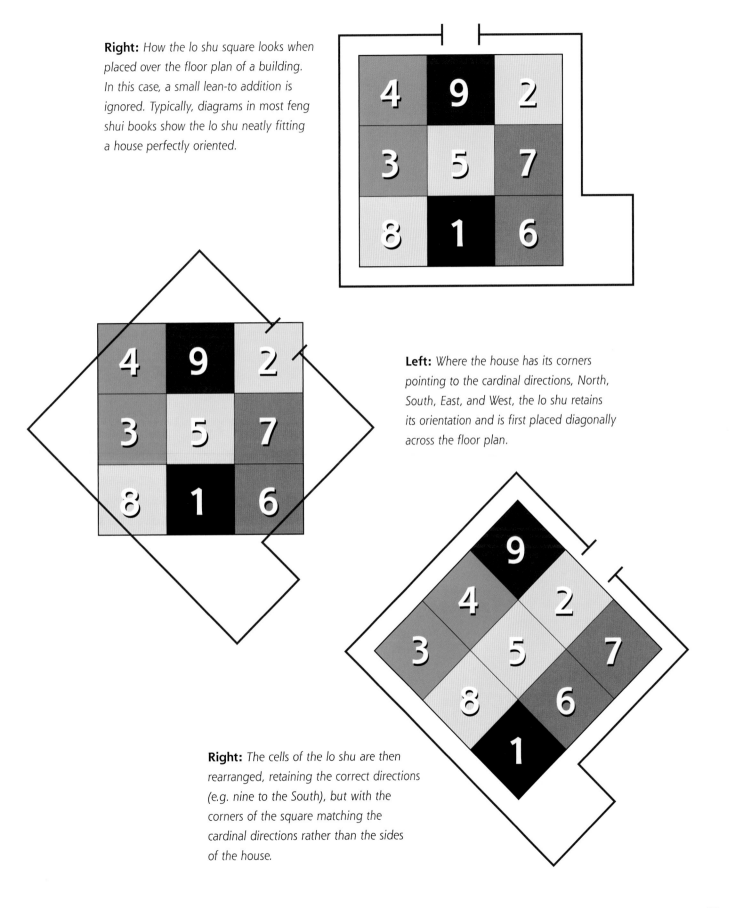

Left: *Where the house has its corners pointing to the cardinal directions, North, South, East, and West, the lo shu retains its orientation and is first placed diagonally across the floor plan.*

Right: *The cells of the lo shu are then rearranged, retaining the correct directions (e.g. nine to the South), but with the corners of the square matching the cardinal directions rather than the sides of the house.*

Your birth year

animal zodiac signs & Elements

Your Chinese animal sign

HOW TO WORK OUT YOUR SIGN

Take the last two digits from the year in which you were born. If the number is greater than 11, subtract 12 from it. Keep subtracting 12 until you have a number less than 12. For example, Nick was born in 1975. His number is greater than 11. So, 75 minus six 12s leaves a remainder of 3. Therefore, Nick's Chinese animal sign is the Rabbit. Do the same with your birth year, and then read off your sign from the table below:

Animal birth year	
0	Rat
1	Ox
2	Tiger
3	Rabbit
4	Dragon
5	Snake
6	Horse
7	Goat (Sheep)
8	Monkey
9	Rooster
10	Dog
11	Pig
12	Rat

(For those born after Chinese New Year in 2000, see main text right).

Not all rooms, homes, or offices are equally lucky for all people. Individuals have different best positions and facing directions, depending on their horoscope. The most basic form of popular Chinese astrology divides everyone up into one of 12 animal signs, according to the year they were born. Whatever anyone says, there is only a very tenuous connection between these animal signs and the 12 signs of the western zodiac. For a start, the twelve western zodiacal signs change from month to month, while one Chinese animal sign will last for a whole year. In fact, the Chinese signs are more related to the 11.86 years it takes Jupiter to rotate around the sun. However, every 12 years the Chinese animal sign completes a full cycle.

Any child born after Chinese New Year in 2000—5 February—but before Chinese New Year in 2001—23 January—will be born under the sign of the Dragon. This is thought to be an excellent sign to be born under. In turn, as the years change, the signs are in succession:

2000	Dragon	2004	Monkey	2008	Rat
2001	Snake	2005	Rooster	2009	Ox
2002	Horse	2006	Dog	2010	Tiger
2003	Goat	2007	Pig	2011	Rabbit

Traditionally, the Rat commences the cycle, as it was thought to be the brightest of all the Signs. In the last century, the Rat held sway in 1912, 1924, 1936, 1948, 1960, 1972, 1984 and 1996.

In more complex Chinese astrology, these 12 Animals are called the 12 Earthly Branches of the year of birth. There is also one of ten Heavenly Stems allocated to your year of birth. These Heavenly Stems don't have the picturesque animal associations of the 12 Earthly Branches, but each Stem and Branch do have an associated Element.

Besides having a Branch and a Stem associated with your year of birth, you also have a Branch and Stem connected with your month,

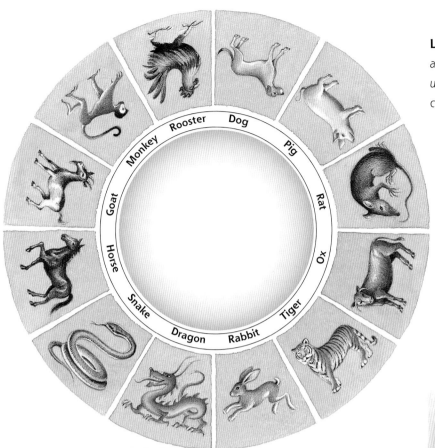

day, and hour of birth. This gives four Branches and four Stems, which, taken together, make up your Four Pillar horoscope.

The calculation of this more complete horoscope is beyond the scope of this book, but there are other sources, such as books and computer software, that will help you do this.

Your Four Pillar horoscope will have 4 + 4 = 8 Elements associated with it. The balance of these Elements is what tells you if you have a balanced or unbalanced grouping of the Elements. For example, if you had an Element balance of three Fire, two Wood, one Earth, and two Metal, it would be obvious that you have an excess of Fire in your nature. This is, in fact, aggravated by the two Wood, which will contribute to producing more Fire, according to the productive cycle of the Elements. In addition, there is no Water, which might have acted as a check on the Fire.

Relating this back to feng shui and the furnishing of your home or office, you should use blues and blacks to strengthen the Water content of your environment, making for more balance. Thus, the Four Pillar horoscope is a very useful insight into your Element balance. Knowing this, you should endeavor to decorate in a way that will make up for any Element deficiencies you have in your nature, to bring more balance to yourself and your life.

Your Element

WORKING OUT YOUR ELEMENT

To work out your Element, take the last digit of your year of birth and refer to the table below. (If your birthday fell before the Chinese New Year, you were born in the previous year for this calculation).

Element of birth year	
0	Metal
1	Metal
2	Water
3	Water
4	Wood
5	Wood
6	Fire
7	Fire
8	Earth
9	Earth

Your magic kua number

Nine Star Ki

It is interesting that a Japanese system called Nine Star Ki, which is derived from the Chinese kua formula, omits to make a differentiation according to sex. Women using it will therefore get a different kua number than if they had used the Chinese system. It is better not to mix these systems and to stay with the traditional Chinese calculations.

Location and kua numbers

Having a kua number of 8 with a sheng ch'i of Southwest must not be confused with the Southwest Location, which is where changes might be made with furnishings to enhance the "romance luck" of the whole household. They are totally different feng shui formulas.

When doing a feng shui makeover, check the positioning of furniture, especially beds and chairs, very carefully, so that all pieces are positioned according to the kua number of the person using them. It is, for example, usually possible for everyone to face their best Direction while eating, simply by allocating chairs around the table to the correct person. This is not unlike the Victorian habit of allocating "head of the table" to the senior male member of the household. In this case "head of the table" means the breadwinner facing in his/her sheng ch'i or best Direction.

The kua number tells you the best Directions to face at your desk, your TV-watching chair, or your bed— i.e., when you are sitting or sleeping for long periods. To work out your best Directions you must calculate what has become known as your kua number. A kua is a Trigram, as we saw on page 22, and everyone has a ruling Trigram or kua according to their sex and year of birth. You can work out your kua number by using the table at the top of the opposite page. When you have calculated your kua number, check the table of fortunate and unfortunate Directions below to see what yours are.

Everyone has four best Directions and four worst Directions, so there is some flexibility in arranging seating, bed, and front door positions. The very best Direction is called the sheng ch'i Direction, and the very worst, the lui sha Direction. There are times when a specific Direction is best: if you are ill, for example, the tien yi or "doctor from Heaven" Direction is best. Someone looking to marry might face their nien yen Direction, which must not be confused with the Southwest Location, which is where changes might be made with the furnishings to enhance the "romance luck" of the whole household.

How to work out your kua number

WOMEN

1 Say that your date of birth is January 16, 1962. To calculate your kua number, check if you were born before the Chinese New Year. This fell on February 5 in 1962, so your birthday belongs in the previous year, 1961.

2 Now add together the last two digits of this year: 6 + 1 = 7

3 Now check if your answer is greater than 9. It's not, so there is no action on this step. (If it had been, you would have needed to add the constituent digits together.)

4 Being female, add 5 to your answer: 7 + 5 = 12.

5 Check if your answer is greater than 9. It is, so add its constituent digits together: 1 + 2 = 3.

6 Your kua number is 3.

MEN

1 Say your date of birth is March 22, 1948. First check if you were born before the Chinese New Year. This fell on February 10 in that year, so your birth year remains unchanged.

2 Now add together the last two digits: 4 + 8 = 12.

3 Now check if your answer is greater than 9. It is, so add the constituent digits together: 1 + 2 = 3.

4 Being male, subtract your answer from 10: 10 − 3 = 7.

5 Your kua number is 7.

CASE STUDY

Let's put these male and female examples into a relationship, calling them Tim and Susan. Looking at their different best and worst Directions (see the table below), it is obvious that they will have to compromise over the direction in which they orient their bed, as Susan's best Directions are the worst one's for Tim, and vice versa. They can, of course, select dining chairs facing in their best, but different, Directions, because they can sit opposite each other.

Susan's best Direction is South (see the table for kua number 3), but for Tim, South is inauspicious. This does not mean that Tim and Susan are incompatible, simply that if they live together they will have to compromise.

Had Susan's kua number been 2 and Tim's 7, their best Directions would have been an almost perfect match, and their worst Directions could have been avoided. For example, Southwest is an excellent Direction for a kua 2 person, while it is also a good Direction for a number 7 person.

Fortunate and unfortunate Directions

Fortune	Best Direction: great prosperity	Relation-ships & family	Health	Mild good fortune	Accidents & frustrations	Mischief & quarrels	Bad fortune	Worst Direction: least fortune
Chinese name	Sheng Ch'i	Nien Yen	Tien Yi	Fu Wei	Ho hai	Wu Kwei	Chueh Ming	Lui Sha
Kua number below	←			→	---------			➡
1	SE	S	E	N	W	NE	SW	NW
2	NE	NW	W	SW	E	SE	N	S
3	S	SE	N	E	SW	NW	W	NE
4	N	E	S	SE	NW	SW	NE	W
Male 5	NE	NW	W	SW	E	SE	N	S
Female 5	SW	W	NW	NE	S	N	SE	E
6	W	SW	NE	NW	SE	E	S	N
7	NW	NE	SW	W	N	S	E	SE
8	SW	W	NW	NE	S	N	SE	E
9	E	N	SE	S	NE	W	NW	SW

Your best Directions

Auspicious Locations

- mild good fortune
- health
- relationships & family
- great prosperity & success

Inauspicious Locations

- accidents & frustrations
- mischief & quarrels
- bad fortune
- least fortune

Above and below: *Using the color coding above and the diagrams below, you can see at a glance which Locations are best for your kua number.*

Not only will your best Directions be beneficial when placing furniture, but they may also give you the edge in those crucial meetings in which facing the right direction will improve your command of the meeting.

For example, if your kua number is one then your best Direction is Southeast. Thus, if there is a round meeting table and a choice of chairs, selecting the chair facing Southeast will give you a psychological advantage in the meeting. Be aware, however, that the physical alignments of the room take precedence over best Directions. Avoid sitting in a chair with its back to the door or window, if you can help it. Even if your kua number is one, a Southeast-facing chair with its back to the door should be avoided. Instead, try to choose from the East-, South-, or North-facing chairs, in that descending order.

Your sheng ch'i is a great direction in which to have your front door. If you are lucky enough to have this configuration, then the "mouth" of your house, the front door, will gulp in large quantities of the ch'i just right for you.

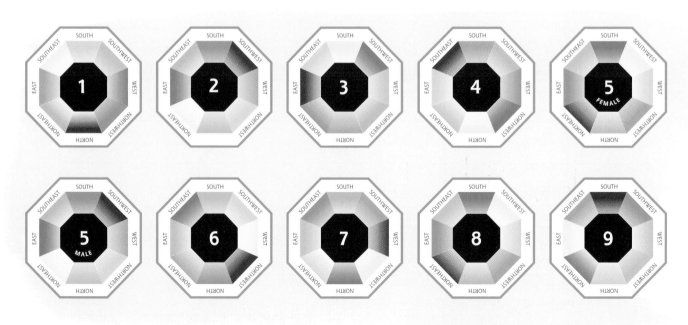

Facing your nien yen Direction will improve relationships between yourself and your family. It will assist in ensuring fertility and in making a good marriage.

Fu wei is a good overall harmony, with a meditation-type peace. It is not so good for getting things done, but promotes happiness.

Your ho hai Direction is the first of your four bad Directions, but it is the mild bad luck of accidents and minor mishaps.

Wu kwei, or literally "five ghosts," promotes sudden bad luck like burglary, fires, being dismissed from your job, or getting into fights: sudden disruption, rather like seeing a ghost.

Finally, the most unlucky Direction is your lui sha Direction. Try not to sleep with your head pointing in this Direction, nor should you work facing this way. A front door facing this Direction will usher in severe bad luck, real loss of wealth or chronic illness. If you face your lui sha Direction for long periods of time, you had better be prepared for legal problems, illness, or more serious accidents. At best, it causes missed opportunities.

East Group houses and West Group houses

If you look carefully at the table on page 31, you will notice that the four best Directions in each kua are grouped either as SE/E/S/N or NE/W/NW/SW, although not necessarily in that order. From this, it can be seen that people fall into one of two categories:

W Those with a "West Life" kua number whose best Directions are NE/W/NW/SW—i.e., West plus three inter-cardinal points.

E Those with an "East Life" kua number whose best Directions are SE/E/S/N—i.e., SE plus three cardinal points.

Look at the first column of the table on page 31, where you will see that kua numbers 1, 3, 4, and 9 are shown as East Life, and kua numbers 2, 5, 6, 7, and 8 are shown as West Life.

Just as people can be categorized as either East Life or West Life, so houses can be categorized as either East Group houses or West Group houses. Obviously East Life people suit East Group houses and West Life people suit West Group houses.

How do you tell which houses are which? Simply by observing the location of the "sitting position," or back door. West Group houses have back doors facing Northeast, West, Northwest and Southwest and are associated with Metal or Earth. East Group houses have back doors facing Southeast, South, North and East and are associated with Water, Wood, or Fire. So if you are a West Life person, try to live in a West Group house.

Above: *West Group houses have back doors facing Northeast, West, Northwest, or Southwest.*

Above: *East Group houses have back doors facing Southeast, East, North, or South.*

2

Practical Applications

Now that we've been through the theory, it's time to apply it in a practical feng shui makeover of your home, office, or garden. Any and every trick of the interior designer's trade can be brought to bear upon a feng shui problem or enhancement.

Some feng shui changes can be brought about simply by changing the decor appropriately, to stress or reduce one or other of the five Elements. This can be done by introducing changes in color, shape, and material, or by actually introducing the physical Element itself, the latter being the most potent.

Color, shape & material

Since the basic Chinese palette is rather stark, variations on its fundamental coloration can be substituted when trying to represent or enhance a particular Element. For example, you might like to use a salmon color (derived from red, white, and yellow) to stimulate the Element Earth.

Fire is attributed to the South, where shades of red and orange are appropriate, but not yellow, which belongs to Earth. Be careful not to use the very yin white here. Sometimes purple is attributed to Fire: in fact this color is more appropriate to Metal. A small amount of green adds an interesting charge (charge is the technical term meaning a small quantity or flash of a contrasting color).

Earth is attributed to the Center, Southwest, and Northeast, and here brown and ocher through to bright yellows are appropriate. As with Fire, for best results, be careful not to use the very yin white here. A small quantity of red adds an interesting galvanizing effect. Never use black or blue.

Wood (East and Southeast) is growing vegetation, and therefore green through to azure are appropriate colors to use in these areas. The blue of water is supportive and strengthening.

COLOR AND SHAPE
To amplify an Element, introduce more of its color, the color of the Element that produces it, or shapes symbolizing that Element.

Color and shape

Element	Fire	Earth	Wood	Metal	Water
Color	Red	Yellow	Green	Metallic	Black or Dark Blue
Color of producing element	Green	Red	Black or Dark Blue	Silver or Gold Yellow	Metallic Silver or Gold
Shape	Triangular, pointed, and sharp	Square, low	Upright rectangles	Domes, arches, circles, spheres	Flowing, wavy or freehand shapes

Material

Element	Fire	Earth	Wood	Metal	Water
May be represented by	Candles, electric light	Rocks, crystals	Growing indoor plants	Metal wind chimes, or any metallic or electronic device	Aquarium, indoor fountain*

MATERIAL

Using the Element itself is by far the best way of accentuating the influence of that particular Element.

* (make sure the water is moving—not stagnant)

Metal (West and Northwest) is an interesting Element, sometimes translated as gold. Hence, colors include gold, silver, and the otherwise very yin white. Purple and silver make an excellent energizing combination in this area. Yellow, representative of the producing Element Earth, is useful here.

Water (North) is traditionally symbolized by black, but blue has found its way on to the palette of Water colors. A touch of gold, representing Water's producing Element Metal, works wonders here. Water is symbolic of money, and so the combination of gold on black has often been used to stimulate the flow of prosperity. Be careful not to use fiery red here, as Water is inimical to Fire.

As well as with colors, each Element may also be stimulated by using its producing Element (see pages 20—21). Fire, for example, may be stimulated by introducing growing indoor plants—i.e., Wood, which feeds Fire.

Finally, the Elements may be represented by pictures, but this is carrying feng shui symbolism too far. It's much better to use color, shape, and material in a way that satisfies both the Element you are attempting to enhance and the associated mood. Remember, you don't have to makeover all of the eight Locations, simply the ones relevant to you now. Also note that these choices might change later.

In addition to colors and materials, shapes can also help symbolize the Elements (see table left). Fire, for example, is represented by anything triangular (apex upward), while Earth appears in low, flat, plateau-like shapes. Wood is characterized by upright rectangles, Water by anything wavy, and Metal by rounded or domed shapes. Now that you have the elements of feng shui makeover, it is up to your ingenuity to apply these to individual rooms, as outlined in the following pages.

Element	Symbolized by
Fire	A picture of flames
Earth	A picture of a formation like Ayers Rock in Australia
Wood	Pictures of growing trees or plants
Metal	Photo of a metallic object
Water	Picture of a mighty river or waterfall

SYMBOLS

If you cannot supply the actual Element, you can substitute a picture, but it will be much less effective at enhancing the Element than actual colors, shapes, and materials.

Front door

Above: *A winding path conducts ch'i gradually to the main door of a building.*

The Direction of the front door matters more than most other feng shui considerations. The front door is considered to be the "mouth" of the house or a commercial building. It is through this that most of the all-important ch'i enters the building. Ch'i also enters the building in other ways—through open windows, for example—but the front door is the most important.

What does this mean for you? Well, the direction in which the door points determines the kind of ch'i that enters the house. We know from reading about the eight Trigrams, the pa kua, that each of the eight Directions is attributed to one of the Trigrams. The sort of ch'i that enters a door facing South is that which is conditioned by the ch'ien or Heaven Trigram (in the Earlier Heaven Sequence). It is strong, masculine yang ch'i and the exact opposite of the ch'i

Right: *The main door of any building is the "mouth" through which that building absorbs most of its ch'i.*

that enters through a door facing North, which will receive the more yin type of ch'i associated with the k'un or Earth Trigram. This is why the direction in which the door faces is most important, and why it affects more advanced feng shui like Flying Star feng shui.

The door itself should be solid, and preferably not punctured by a vulnerable glass panel—for crime prevention as well as feng shui reasons.

The next thing you should do is check to see if any alignment is aimed at your front door, generating "poison arrows." A "poison arrow" is created where ch'i is able to gather momentum up a long straight street, for example. If such a configuration exists pointing toward the front door, try to deflect it with a hedge, or something similar to block it. If this fails and the "poison arrow" is caused by a major alignment, then hang an octagonal pa kua mirror over your door, pointing in the offending direction, to send back the sha ch'i whence it came.

Never just hang pa kua mirrors up for fun, and certainly never inside your home or office. If this fails too, a more drastic step is to re-orient the whole front door, but this has other impacts on the feng shui of the building and should be done only with expert advice.

The front door:
- Should open onto an uncramped hall space containing no clutter.
- Should not face a bathroom door.
- Should not face a mirror, which will deflect good ch'i entering the building directly out again.
- Should not lead into a hall that passes straight through the house and out of the back door, otherwise the ch'i entering will be immediately conducted out of the house again without benefiting the occupants. If this is the case, hang wind chimes or place potted plants in the hall to deflect or slow down the ch'i.
- Should not have obstructions that prevent it from fully opening and therefore letting in the maximum amount of beneficial ch'i.
- Should not have a bathroom on the floor directly above, or in the foyer immediately inside it, as this will taint the ch'i entering the building.

Above: *Aligning the front gate, path, and main door is a common feng shui fault in many houses.*

Remember that the outside of a building is governed by the Earlier Heaven Sequence of the Trigrams, not the Later Heaven Sequence of Trigrams that applies to the interior of the building.

Front door — bad feng shui

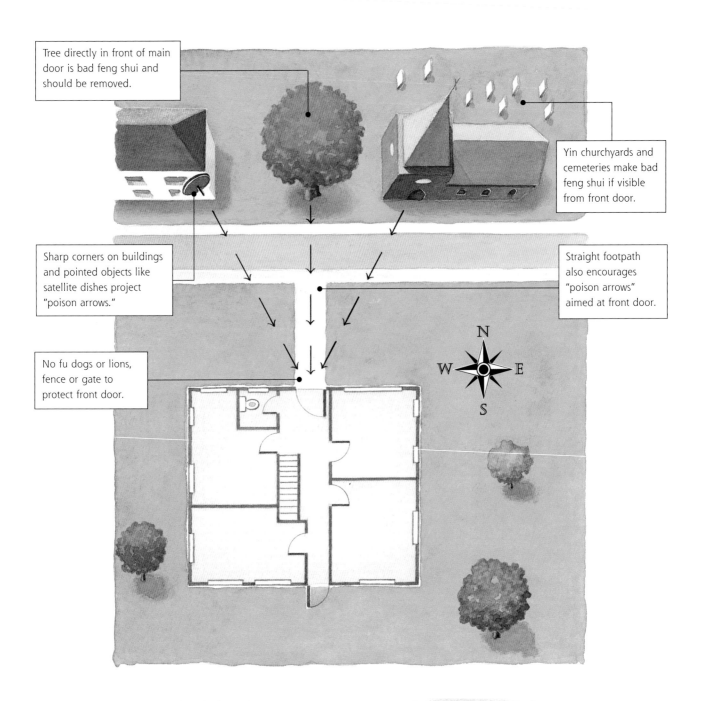

Tree directly in front of main door is bad feng shui and should be removed.

Yin churchyards and cemeteries make bad feng shui if visible from front door.

Sharp corners on buildings and pointed objects like satellite dishes project "poison arrows."

Straight footpath also encourages "poison arrows" aimed at front door.

No fu dogs or lions, fence or gate to protect front door.

The siting of this house is unfortunate because of the influence of objects visible from the front door that creates bad feng shui. The church, tree and house on the other side of the road all project "secret arrows" at the front door, and the graveyard, being very yin, makes bad feng shui visible from the front door. The front door itself is also completely unprotected from the "poison arrows" pointed at it, and there is no ming tang (an open area at the front of a building) for the collection of ch'i.

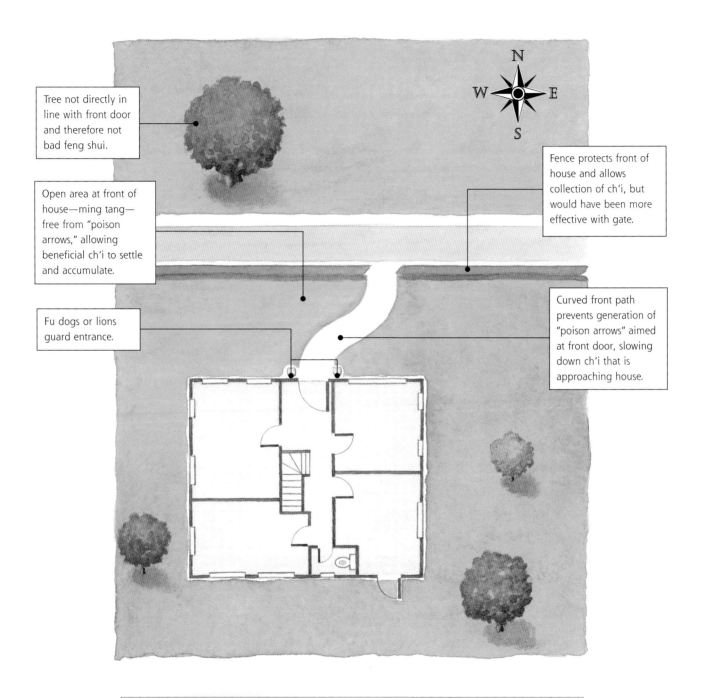

Tree not directly in line with front door and therefore not bad feng shui.

Open area at front of house—ming tang— free from "poison arrows," allowing beneficial ch'i to settle and accumulate.

Fu dogs or lions guard entrance.

Fence protects front of house and allows collection of ch'i, but would have been more effective with gate.

Curved front path prevents generation of "poison arrows" aimed at front door, slowing down ch'i that is approaching house.

This time the house is in a much better position. It has an open aspect to the front, which means that nothing is projecting "secret arrows" at the front door. It also has a curved front path to slow down ch'i as it approaches the house, and a ming tang area behind the fence, in which the ch'i can collect before entering the house. The fu dogs and the fence both guard the entrance to the house, but the absence of a gate makes the fence less effective in this role than it might otherwise have been.

Hall & stairs

Above: *A well-lit front hall encourages the entry of ch'i.*

Since the front door is perhaps the most important feng shui feature, being the mouth of the house, through which most of the ch'i enters, so the hall directly inside the door is also very important. Ideally the hall should be well lit to encourage the entry of ch'i.

A hall that is a "through" hall, passing directly to the back door is bad feng shui, as ch'i will pass straight through the house without accumulating. In such a case add decorative features like indoor plants or a hall table to deflect the ch'i from its direct path. Another cure is to hang wind chimes from the ceiling of the hall to slow the passage of the ch'i.

Corridors and stairs are very similar from a feng shui point of view, both being narrow passages from one part of the house to another. The only difference is that stairs are inclined passages. Like halls, which carry the ch'i from one room to another, stairs distribute the ch'i from one floor to another.

Right: *In this hall the curved table and the mirror facing away from the door are good, but the umbrella stand immediately inside the door causes problems because the chair behind it prevents the door from being opened fully, and so stops beneficial ch'i from entering the house.*

In many western houses the staircase often follows on almost directly after a short stretch of hall. This allows ch'i to come in the front door and rush straight up the stairs. This is not advisable—remember, the best ch'i flows slowly and not in direct straight lines. The makeover solution to this problem is the hanging of wind chimes between the door and the stairs to slow down the ch'i. Ideally the staircase should turn away from the front door: certain commercial buildings have been deliberately designed to incorporate this architectural feature.

On staircases where the ch'i cannot be coaxed up in sufficient quantities to enliven the upstairs rooms, it is sometimes useful to place stronger lights on the staircase itself, or, in extreme cases, an object resembling a barber's pole on a landing. This turns in a spiral fashion and promotes the movement of ch'i up the stairs.

Paradoxically, although ch'i should be encouraged to move in a circular fashion, spiral staircases are not considered good feng shui because they act like screwdrivers, accelerating ch'i down into the lower room. Rapidly rushing ch'i is never good, so avoid spiral staircases wherever possible.

General rules

- Long corridors leading from the front door are bad news and should, if possible, be screened off or interrupted with the hanging of wind chimes.
- The front door should not face a staircase directly, particularly not one leading downward. To open on to both descending and ascending stairs is the very worst configuration, and some type of screen or baffle should be introduced just inside the door.
- Halls should not be dark and yin but bright and yang, as they conduct ch'i from one part of the house to another.
- Three doorways or windows in a row are considered very bad feng shui and should have wind chimes or a beaded curtain suspended to disperse the ch'i, which might otherwise become a "poison arrow."
- Doors facing each other across a corridor should be the same size. If they are different, even up the width of the doorways by hanging a vertical mirror strip, for example.
- Poorly lit or low-ceilinged stairs can oppress and restrict ch'i flow between floors. Try using a bright light to enhance circulation, or possibly put a mirror on the ceiling, which will give the appearance of the hall being heightened.

Above: *Turning staircases, as long as they are not spiral, are better feng shui than one straight, precipitous descent.*

Above: *Spiral staircases encourage ch'i to move too fast down into the lower room and are therefore not good feng shui.*

Hall & stairs — bad feng shui

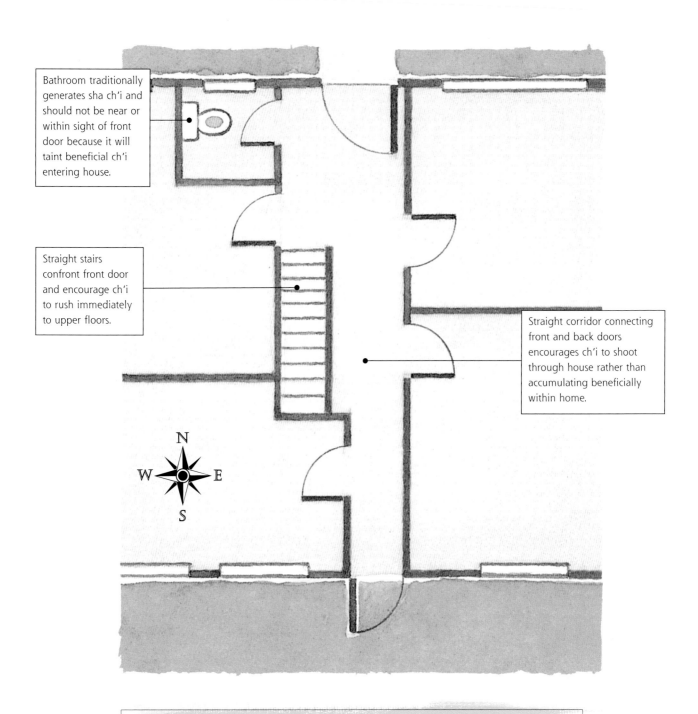

Bathroom traditionally generates sha ch'i and should not be near or within sight of front door because it will taint beneficial ch'i entering house.

Straight stairs confront front door and encourage ch'i to rush immediately to upper floors.

Straight corridor connecting front and back doors encourages ch'i to shoot through house rather than accumulating beneficially within home.

In this house the straight, unobstructed corridor connecting front and back doors encourages beneficial ch'i entering at the "mouth" of the house—the street door—to rush straight through the house. In addition, the bathroom is visible from the front door, and the straight stairs descend from the second floor for a head-on confrontation with the front door. All in all, very bad feng shui.

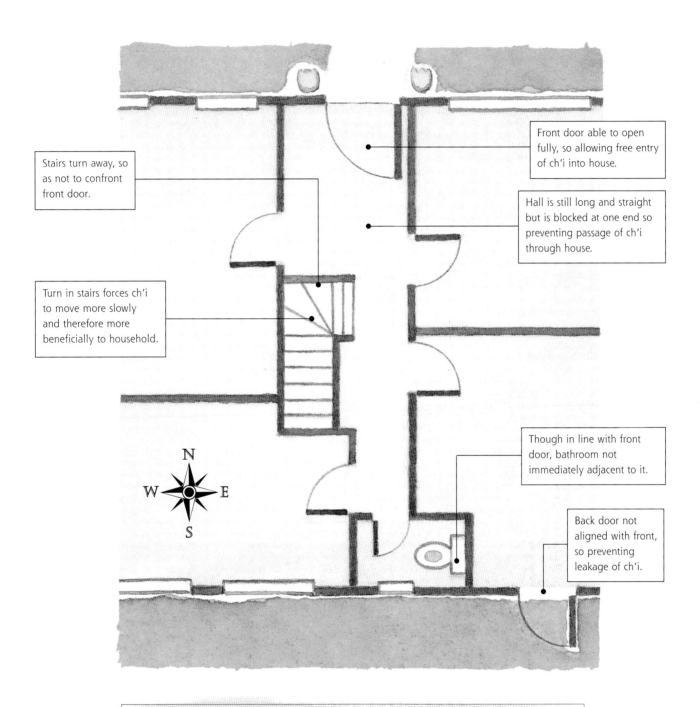

Stairs turn away, so as not to confront front door.

Front door able to open fully, so allowing free entry of ch'i into house.

Hall is still long and straight but is blocked at one end so preventing passage of ch'i through house.

Turn in stairs forces ch'i to move more slowly and therefore more beneficially to household.

Though in line with front door, bathroom not immediately adjacent to it.

Back door not aligned with front, so preventing leakage of ch'i.

N
W · E
S

Though the hall is still long and straight, it is now blocked at one end, preventing ch'i escaping. The front door opens fully to allow the maximum amount of ch'i to enter the house. The bathroom is not now visible from the front door, although its door still is. A mirror, or mirrored tiles, could be hung here, seemingly making the door "disappear." The stairs turn away from a head-on confrontation with the front door, and ch'i is encouraged to move upstairs in its natural mode—i.e., gently circulating. Using warm yellow wall colors will increase the welcoming feeling in this part of the building.

Kitchen

Above: *A preparation island in the middle of the room violates the feng shui principle that the central tai ch'i of any room should be open and empty.*

The kitchen is a very special place because it is where your meals are prepared. In feng shui, food symbolizes nourishment and, by extension, health and wealth. Just as we take care over hygiene when working in a kitchen, so we should take care of the feng shui of the place where our food is prepared.

General rules

- Since the oven is symbolic of the Element Fire, and the sink and refrigerator symbolic of Water, you should be careful in kitchen design that these two not clash. For example, the sink and cooker should not confront each other. Similarly they should not be located next to each other; at right angles is fine.
- The "mouth" of the oven should not face a door opening.
- Preparation surfaces should be located so that the cook should not have his or her back to the kitchen door while working.
- The kitchen itself should be in a protected part of the house and not be immediately visible from the front door.
- Try to use green in the decor of the kitchen, since Wood, which green represents, supports Fire and is supported by Water, both of which will inevitably be present in a kitchen.
- Don't put up mirrors facing the oven, as the doubling of Fire may pose a fire threat to the household.
- A preparation island in the middle of the kitchen is not good feng shui, as the central tai ch'i should remain open and empty.
- The kitchen should not be beneath a bathroom on the floor above, and preferably not under any "wet" rooms, such as a shower room.
- The kitchen should not be located in the Northwest corner of the house as this is the corner associated with the Heaven Trigram ch'ien, thus resulting in "Fire at Heaven's gate," a feng shui configuration which is very undesirable.

One of the most important rules is connected with the orientation of the oven mouth. Ideally it should coincide with the kua number of the breadwinner or their partner. Use the instructions on page 31 to calculate your kua number and the table on the left to check the best oven Direction.

Best oven mouth Directions

KUA NUMBER	DIRECTION
1	E
2	W
3	N
4	S
5	W (male)
	or NW (female)
6	NE
7	SW
8	NW
9	SE

At the very least, try not to have the oven mouth facing any of your four worst Directions. The definition of oven mouth is controversial in the case of electric ranges, some experts claiming it is the direction of the plug, or source of fuel. More probably, it is the facing direction of the door from which the food emerges.

Since the oven is the source of the family's food and hence well-being, it should be well protected from any inauspicious configurations, such as conflict with Water in the form of the sink or the refrigerator.

Paradoxically, because the kitchen is a "wet" room and therefore drains away ch'i, it is quite good if it is located in that part of the home which corresponds to one of your worst Locations. Alternatively, it is acceptable if it is located in one of the eight Aspirations (see page 23), which are unimportant to you, for example West (meaning children) for someone who does not have or particularly want children. Of course, this is a counsel of perfection and hard to organize unless you are building your house from scratch.

Above: *The kitchen is probably the most complex room in the house to makeover from a feng shui perspective.*

Kitchen — bad feng shui

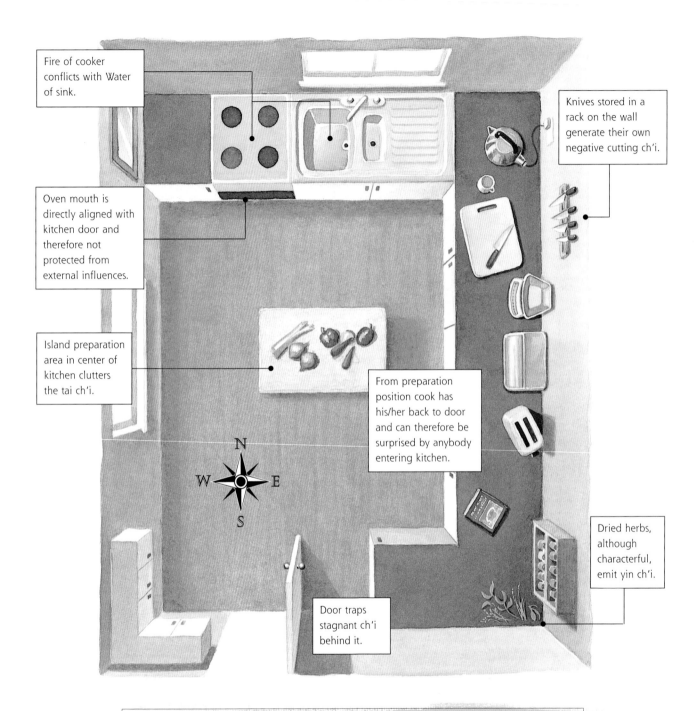

Fire of cooker conflicts with Water of sink.

Knives stored in a rack on the wall generate their own negative cutting ch'i.

Oven mouth is directly aligned with kitchen door and therefore not protected from external influences.

Island preparation area in center of kitchen clutters the tai ch'i.

From preparation position cook has his/her back to door and can therefore be surprised by anybody entering kitchen.

Dried herbs, although characterful, emit yin ch'i.

Door traps stagnant ch'i behind it.

In this kitchen the two key features—the sink and the cooker—are next to each other, so their Elements—Fire and Water—come into direct conflict. The oven mouth faces straight out of the open door and is therefore not protected from external influences. The door itself opens on to dead space, behind which stagnant ch'i collects. In the center of the room the island preparation area clutters up the tai ch'i, while the cook, when facing the worktop, has his/her back to the door and can therefore be surprised by someone coming into the room.

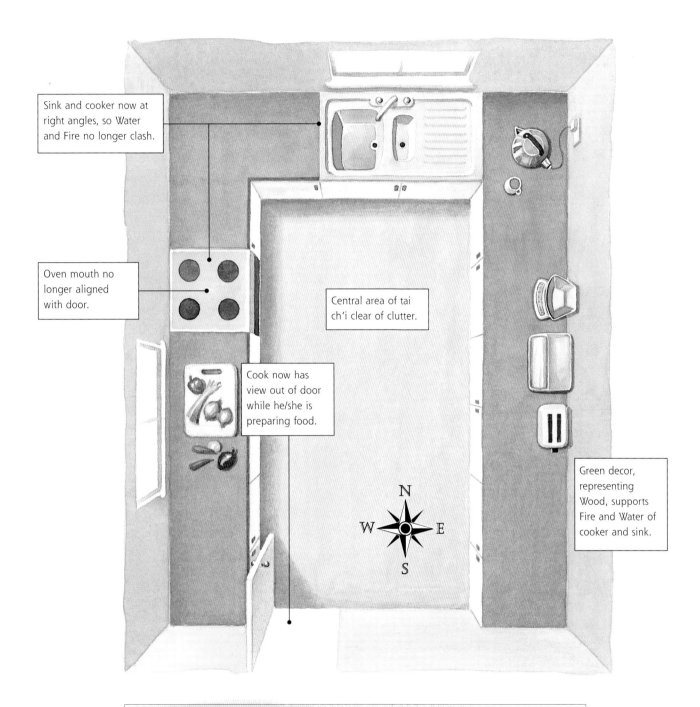

Sink and cooker now at right angles, so Water and Fire no longer clash.

Oven mouth no longer aligned with door.

Central area of tai ch'i clear of clutter.

Cook now has view out of door while he/she is preparing food.

Green decor, representing Wood, supports Fire and Water of cooker and sink.

N
W E
S

The sink and cooker are now at right angles, so the two Elements they represent no longer clash. The oven door no longer faces out of the kitchen door—a very bad feng shui alignment. The cook is much happier because he/she can both see out of the window and through the open doorway, so avoiding unpleasant surprises. The knives which emitted cutting ch'i have been put away in a drawer and the dried herbs have been removed so that they no longer emit yin ch'i.

Living room

Hi-fi systems and TVs

Hi-fi systems, computers, and TVs are all considered as belonging to the Metal Element, so ideally should be positioned on the West or Northwest (Metal) sides of the room. The sound and light that come out of them also make them yang, in fact too yang for yin rooms like the bedroom. Try also to avoid making the TV the focus of the room.

The living room is the focus of family activities and, after the kitchen, one of the most used rooms in any house. The pa kua, with its division of the room into the eight Aspirations, can be applied either to the whole house or to a single room. Some rooms have specific no-nos: for example, although water cures any predominantly over-yang items or areas, it should not be used in the bedroom. In particular, you should avoid stimulating the "wet" rooms of the house: the kitchen or bathroom.

Often, because of the specific restrictions on these rooms, the living room can become the main room for the installation of feng shui-related improvements. The living room thus becomes a microcosm of the whole house, with changes made here affecting the feng shui of the entire household.

General rules

- Make sure that the general design is such that there are no cut-off corners where ch'i can stagnate.
- Try to arrange the chairs so that none have their backs to the doorway.
- Look to see if you, and indeed ch'i, can move easily through the room without bumping into furniture or catching on sharp edges.
- Minimize any sharp edges that might create "secret arrows" by draping them or allowing indoor plants to cover them.
- Try to avoid L-shaped furniture configurations. Sharp edges include the right-angled protruding corners that will always be found in any L-shaped rooms.
- Make sure that the room is reasonably lit—the living room needs to be more yang than yin.
- To stimulate conversation and interest in other things, try not to design the room so that the TV is the focus. It is a common modern design habit to focus the room on the TV, just as in past times the focus used to be the hearth.
- Try to position the TV and hi-fi on the West or Northwest (Metal) sides of the room.
- If there are multiple entrances, thought should be given to the flow of ch'i through the room so that one entrance becomes the main one.

- Chairs should not be placed in "confrontational" positions—i.e., directly facing each other, except over the dining table. Try to position them at 90- or 45-degree angles to each other.
- Try to avoid placing any chairs under any overhead beams. If you can't avoid beams, attach ch'i conductors—like flutes—to them to allow ch'i concentrations to drain harmlessly away.
- Try to orient any chair regularly used by a specific member of the family to watch TV in a Direction that is one of the best for that family member.
- The general yin/yang balance of the room should be checked, so if there is much dark heavy furniture (yin), this should be balanced by light, bright hangings, wall colors or lighting.
- Bookcases or shelves, particularly glass shelves, act like knife blades, generating cutting ch'i, so these should be minimized, if possible, with remedies such as providing doors to all open shelves.
- A chandelier positioned centrally in this room is very good feng shui, because it introduces much yang light. Also, because it is symbolic of Fire in the Production Cycle of the Elements, it produces Earth, which is the Element of the central square of the pa kua.

Above: *This conventional living room suffers from a very square, formal look focused on the fireplace.*

Below: *A central chandelier in a living room is good feng shui.*

Living room — bad feng shui

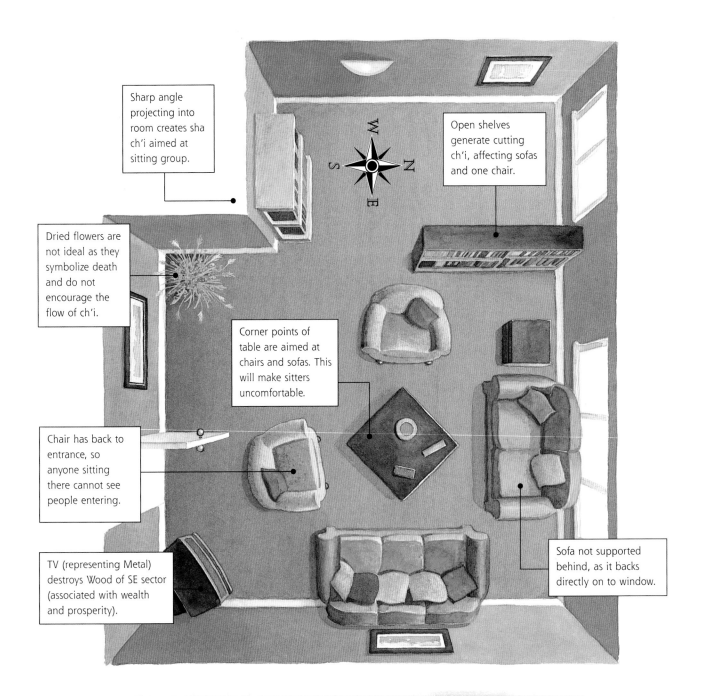

Sharp angle projecting into room creates sha ch'i aimed at sitting group.

Open shelves generate cutting ch'i, affecting sofas and one chair.

Dried flowers are not ideal as they symbolize death and do not encourage the flow of ch'i.

Corner points of table are aimed at chairs and sofas. This will make sitters uncomfortable.

Chair has back to entrance, so anyone sitting there cannot see people entering.

TV (representing Metal) destroys Wood of SE sector (associated with wealth and prosperity).

Sofa not supported behind, as it backs directly on to window.

In this room people seated on the sofa and easy chairs have sha and cutting ch'i coming at them from several different directions: from the sharp angle projecting into the room, the open shelves in the bookshelf, and the pointed corners of the coffee table. Other problems are the window behind the sofa, which deprives the sofa of necessary support, and the TV in the Southeast corner, which destroys the Wood Element (representing wealth and prosperity) normally associated with this sector.

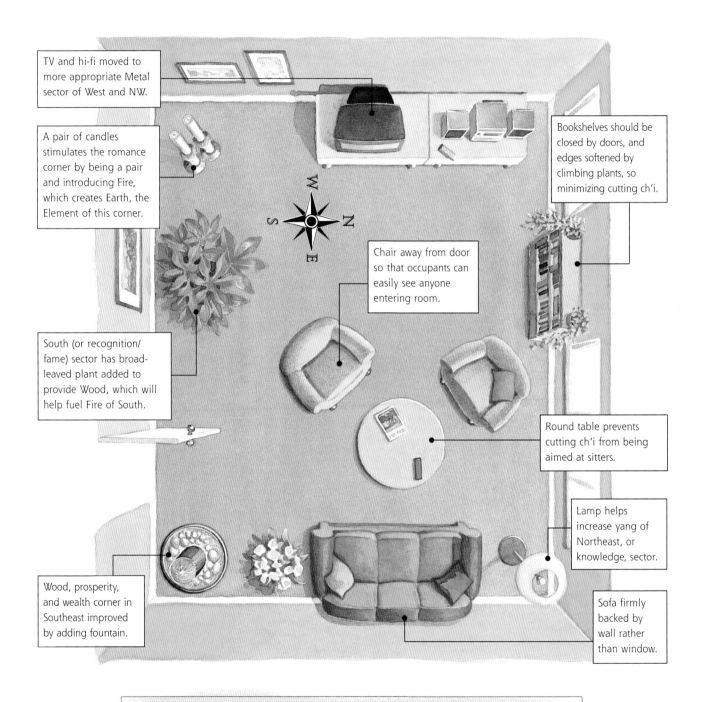

TV and hi-fi moved to more appropriate Metal sector of West and NW.

A pair of candles stimulates the romance corner by being a pair and introducing Fire, which creates Earth, the Element of this corner.

South (or recognition/ fame) sector has broad-leaved plant added to provide Wood, which will help fuel Fire of South.

Bookshelves should be closed by doors, and edges softened by climbing plants, so minimizing cutting ch'i.

Chair away from door so that occupants can easily see anyone entering room.

Round table prevents cutting ch'i from being aimed at sitters.

Lamp helps increase yang of Northeast, or knowledge, sector.

Wood, prosperity, and wealth corner in Southeast improved by adding fountain.

Sofa firmly backed by wall rather than window.

Following a major overhaul, the room has been squared up and rearranged to improve feng shui. None of the seats is now affected by cutting ch'i, the TV has been moved to a sector more appropriate to its Element (Metal), and the wealth, prosperity and knowledge sectors have been strengthened by Wood and lighting respectively. Also, a broad-leaved plant representing Wood has been put against the South wall to fuel the Fire of the South and energize the recognition/fame sectors. The walls are now a warm yellow color; this is more welcoming for visitors and encourages conversation.

Dining room

Above: *A dining room mirror symbolically doubles the quantity of food on the table and, therefore, the household's wealth.*

INDIVIDUAL POSITIONING

- *Selecting the correct seat at the dining room table is important.*
- *There is an ideal format which suggests a round or octagonal table, with each member of the household seated in the position occupied by their Trigram in the Later Heaven Sequence. For example, the male head of the household should sit in the Northwest—the position occupied by the ch'ien or Heaven Trigram; the mother in the Southwest, where the k'un Trigram falls, while the youngest daughter should sit in the West by the tui Trigram.*
- *Another, more practical, arrangement is to have everyone facing one of their four best Directions, especially their sheng ch'i, if at all possible.*

The dining room is where you gather, with either family or friends, to eat together. As already mentioned, in the Chinese world of feng shui, eating well and prosperity are closely linked in a way that does not occur in the West. The famous multi-course meals of Chinese banquet fame are an example of this belief. The larger the number of courses, so symbolically the greater the apparent prosperity of the family giving the banquet.

This concept is reflected in the practice of feng shui by recommendations that the quantity of food on the dining table be symbolically doubled by placing a mirror opposite the table. The mirror, however, must not reflect another mirror on the opposite wall. Mirrors reflecting each other into infinity exhaust and confuse the ch'i. You have only to stand in the middle of a configuration like this and immediately you will feel uncomfortable. Try also not to position the mirror so that it appears to cut off the heads of diners. This is not to be encouraged, even symbolically.

Where the dining room is open-plan with the kitchen, you have particular difficulties, because the function and status of these two rooms is dramatically different. Water, fire, and drainage are unavoidable in a kitchen and yet should not be a part of a dining room. You should therefore be careful to make sure that none of the strong Elements present in a kitchen affects the dining part of the room. Also, don't use a mirror to reflect the food unless you are sure that it does not reflect the fire of the oven, and try not to have the oven facing directly into the dining area.

General rules

- Because the dining room is central to the nourishment of the household, it should ideally be a room close to the center of the home. It certainly should not open directly on to the street, or on to public areas.
- If the house is multistory, try to ensure that the dining room table is not located directly under a toilet on the floor above. Obviously it's not good to have the source of the family's nourishment pressed down upon by foul water. To a lesser extent, the dining room should not be beneath a bathroom at all or beneath a kitchen, for the same reason.

- The energy in this room should be predominantly yang (as opposed to the bedroom, which should be predominantly yin). Hence, decoration should be with positive colors: red, pink, yellow, orange, or bright green.

- If the dining room is located at the center of the home, an area associated with the Element Earth, yellows and earth tones would be the most appropriate colors.

- If possible, no chairs should show their backs in the direction of the doorway to the dining room.

- Do not allow the dining table to be oppressed by overhead beams, or large, heavy chandeliers. Overhead beams can be disguised with tenting so long as this is not itself oppressive.

- Any paintings in the room should show food or other "good fortune" subjects. In the context of Chinese culture, paintings of peaches or oranges are considered to be fortunate.

- If there are different floor levels in a home, try to arrange things, so that the dining room is higher that the surrounding rooms. In this way beneficial ch'i will penetrate the rest of the home.

- Try to arrange items on the table so that all members of the family have a clear view of each other. The practice in old-fashioned homes or restaurants of having a heavy centerpiece containing flowers or condiments should be avoided.

- Keep the decorating mood upbeat. Try to minimize the use of antiques and other potential sources of yin energy in this room.

- The dining room should not open directly on to one of the "wet" rooms of the house, such as the bathroom, or even the kitchen. This is because these areas of water drainage can deplete the ch'i of the dining room. Of course, common health regulations often forbid a bathroom from opening directly on to the dining room.

- It is even advisable for the dining room not to share a common wall with a bathroom.

- The dining table should ideally be round or have rounded corners.

- The number of people sitting down to eat is governed by complex numerological rules, difficult to legislate for in practice. The most basic rule is to try not to set a dining room table for just four people, as it is an unlucky number in China.

Above: *In this dining room the round table is good feng shui, but the over-large centerpiece hides diners from each other.*

Below: *A central light fixture is good feng shui, so long as it is not too heavy and overbearing.*

Dining room — bad feng shui

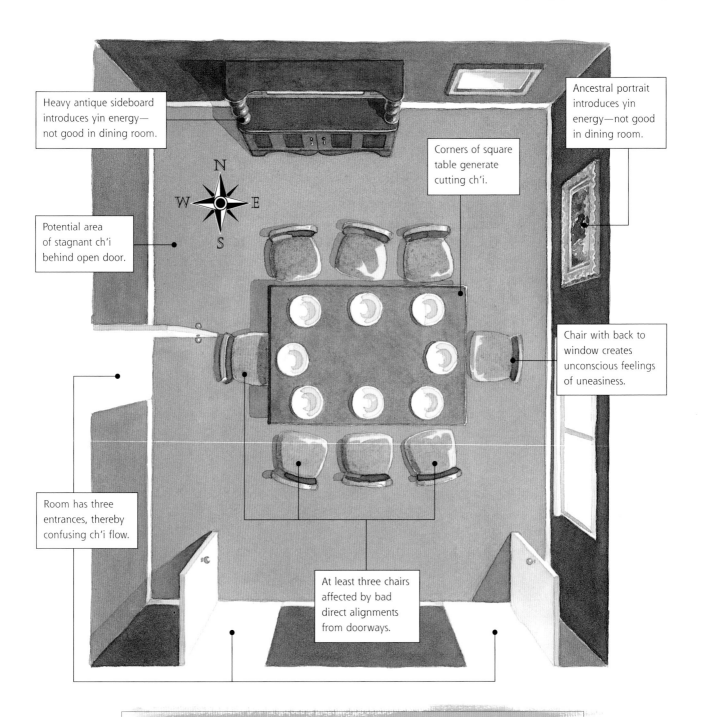

Heavy antique sideboard introduces yin energy—not good in dining room.

Ancestral portrait introduces yin energy—not good in dining room.

Corners of square table generate cutting ch'i.

Potential area of stagnant ch'i behind open door.

Chair with back to window creates unconscious feelings of uneasiness.

Room has three entrances, thereby confusing ch'i flow.

At least three chairs affected by bad direct alignments from doorways.

This room is badly affected by the three doors, which confuse the flow of ch'i and create dead space where stagnant ch'i can collect. Also, this amount of doors means that half of the eight dining chairs are badly aligned, as they have their backs to at least one door. The antique furniture and ancestral portrait introduce yin energy, which is not good for the dining room, and the sharp corners of the dining table send out cutting ch'i.

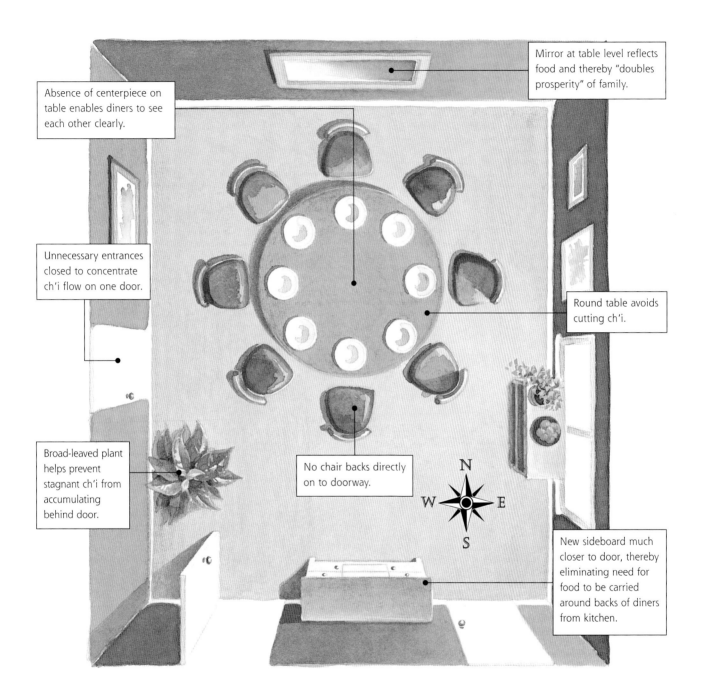

Mirror at table level reflects food and thereby "doubles prosperity" of family.

Absence of centerpiece on table enables diners to see each other clearly.

Unnecessary entrances closed to concentrate ch'i flow on one door.

Round table avoids cutting ch'i.

Broad-leaved plant helps prevent stagnant ch'i from accumulating behind door.

No chair backs directly on to doorway.

New sideboard much closer to door, thereby eliminating need for food to be carried around backs of diners from kitchen.

Closing off two out of the three doors has had a big effect. No diners back directly on to the door, and the ch'i flow is much more concentrated. A broad-leaved plant prevents stagnant ch'i from collecting behind the open door, and a repositioned sideboard means that food no longer has to be carried from the kitchen around the backs of diners. On the other side of the room, a well-placed mirror reflects the food and therefore "doubles the prosperity" of the family. The walls are now a warmer, brighter color, encouraging conversation.

Bathroom

Water is a significant part of feng shui, indeed "water" or "shui" is half the meaning of the term. The designing of exterior waterworks, especially ponds and fountains, has always been an important part of feng shui.

Early feng shui practitioners used hydraulic engineers to redirect the course of whole rivers. Often they imposed some amazing and unnatural patterns on the rivers in an effort to build up and accumulate good ch'i. The reason for all this effort was that water carried ch'i. But water can not only carry ch'i to a site and help store it when it is there, it can also carry it away. Feng shui practitioners working on gardens or landscapes were, therefore, always careful to ensure that the eventual exit point of water—for example, where a river disappeared from view—was invisible from the home.

Below: *Old-fashioned bathtubs allow the drainage system to be visible—bad feng shui.*

These principles carry into the "wet" rooms of the house, where drains carry away ch'i. Hence, you have to be very careful that drains not be open or visible from the home or office. The extension of this rule is that bathroom doors should always be kept closed. Some practitioners have gone to great lengths to fill interior drains with pebbles to hide them. It is not necessary to go quite this far. Just keep the doors of the "wet" rooms closed, and the toilet seat down. In feng shui the toilet is said to create sha ch'i, bad ch'i energy.

Bathrooms containing toilets—as opposed, for example, to a small shower room—are considered an especially problematical kind of "wet" room, because bad smells have always been associated with sha ch'i. The general principle is that, ideally, toilets should be in a location where they do the least damage. In fact, there is positive benefit in having the bathroom in a sector that you want to deplete rather than energize. For example, it might be acceptable to have the bathroom in the West, which is associated with children, if the residents in the home do not have children and are not interested in having them. If, however, the bathroom occurs in a part of the home or office that is important to the occupants, then instead of putting various "cures" in the bathroom, as recommended by some practitioners, you should instead concentrate upon making the toilet "disappear" by keeping the lid down, keeping the door closed, and generally de-emphasizing this room. Use a full-length mirror on the outside of the bathroom door, so that the room's presence will tend to be overlooked.

Above: *Open doors to connecting bathrooms drain valuable ch'i from bedrooms.*

General rules

- Don't have a bathroom positioned so that it is visible from the front door. This is a very bad feng shui configuration.
- Bathrooms should not, for preference, be located in the Northwest or Southeast of any home or office. Location in the Southeast, for example, drains accumulated prosperity.
- Try not to have bathrooms positioned on an upper floor directly above anything except another bathroom or a seldom-used storeroom. The sha ch'i will affect the room below.
- With a connecting bathroom you must be very careful to keep a clear break between the "wet" room and your bedroom, otherwise the energy present in the bedroom can be severely drained, with ill effects for the sleeper's feng shui and health.
- Bathrooms should not be energized, as this just increases sha ch'i.
- Don't use excessive mirrors in the bathroom, as they help to activate the negative effects of the toilet.

Best toilet-facing Directions

KUA NUMBER	DIRECTION
1	SW, NW, NE
2	N, SE, S
3	W, NW, NE
4	SW, W, NE
5 (male)	N, SE, S
5 (female)	N, E, SE
6	N, E, S
7	E, SE, S
8	N, E, SE
9	SW, W, NW

Bathroom — **bad feng shui**

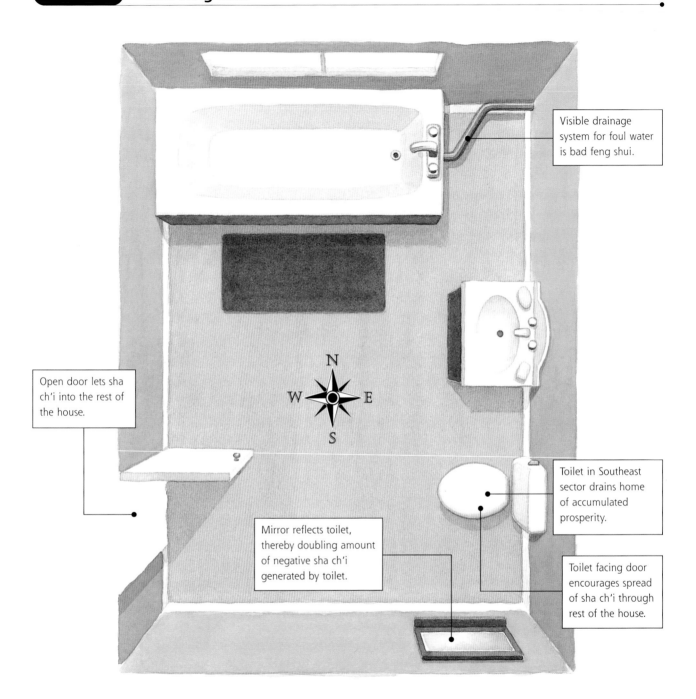

Visible drainage system for foul water is bad feng shui.

Open door lets sha ch'i into the rest of the house.

Toilet in Southeast sector drains home of accumulated prosperity.

Mirror reflects toilet, thereby doubling amount of negative sha ch'i generated by toilet.

Toilet facing door encourages spread of sha ch'i through rest of the house.

The main problem with this bathroom is that the toilet faces directly out of the bathroom door. Toilets are notorious generators of sha ch'i. In this case, a mirror next to the toilet doubles the amount of sha ch'i being generated. The open door directly opposite then encourages this sha ch'i to spread into the rest of the house. Another problem is the pipework coming out of the bath. Anything showing water escaping—and taking ch'i with it—is considered bad feng shui.

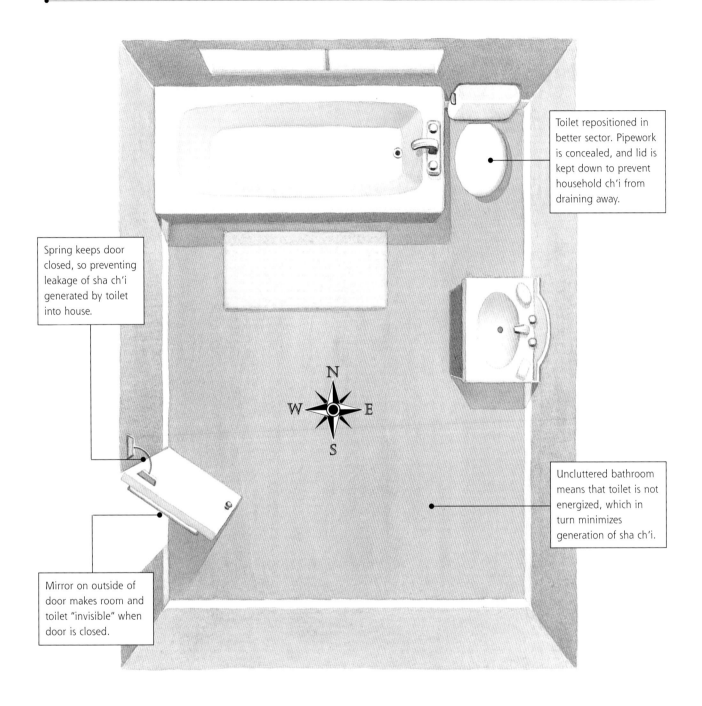

Toilet repositioned in better sector. Pipework is concealed, and lid is kept down to prevent household ch'i from draining away.

Spring keeps door closed, so preventing leakage of sha ch'i generated by toilet into house.

Uncluttered bathroom means that toilet is not energized, which in turn minimizes generation of sha ch'i.

Mirror on outside of door makes room and toilet "invisible" when door is closed.

The bathroom is now in a much more healthy state with the toilet in a better sector and not facing the door. The bathtub drainage pipes have been concealed. A spring has been fitted to the door to keep it closed, thus keeping any bad ch'i in this room. A mirror has been fitted to the outside of the door to "hide" the bathroom and toilet from the rest of the house. The fact that the bathroom is uncluttered means that the toilet is not energized, thus minimizing generation of sha ch'i. When choosing your new wall colors, note that pastels are good feng shui for the bathroom.

Bedroom

Above: *A window behind a headboard is bad feng shui because it leaves the headboard unsupported, and so the person sleeping there is not protected.*

The bedroom is one of the key rooms for feng shui, because we spend about a third of our life there. Therefore the direction in which we orient our bed is very important. Everyone who has slept in different hotels will know that in the morning you can either wake feeling much more rested than you ever do at home or wake feeling as though you are fit for nothing. Barring the bed itself, or the state of the air-conditioning, this huge difference is often the result of sleeping in a non-conducive Direction.

As we saw on page 14, the body responds to the magnetic field of the earth, even at a cellular level. Hence the direction of alignment of the bed is very important. A bedroom should be a place of rest, and predominantly yin. As such, the bedroom should not be too heavily activated with feng shui "cures."

First, if you have a choice of bedrooms choose one in a part of your home that corresponds to one of your best Directions. For example, someone with a kua number of two would do well to choose as their bedroom a room in the Northeast of their home, as that is their sheng ch'i Direction.

General rules
- Don't sleep directly under a beam, as descending ch'i, subconsciously posing a threat above your sleeping head, will disturb your sleep. A four-poster bed, provided it is covered in cloth, does not have such a strong effect.
- Hang a red and gold "double happiness" calligraphy in the bedroom to strengthen your relationship or marriage.
- Don't sleep under overhanging built-in cabinets—these are very bad feng shui.
- Make sure that you can see the door from the bed, so that nobody can come into the room unobserved.
- Don't position the bed with your feet pointing directly out of the door, or so that the bed is in a straight line between the door and a window.
- Make sure you have adequate support behind the headboard; avoid putting the headboard beneath a window, as this removes its support.

- Don't place indoor plants in the bedroom, as they are quite yang.
- The door to the bedroom should not line up directly with a staircase, as that will entail a strong ch'i flow into or out of the bedroom. If this is unavoidable, use a very strong uplight just outside the door.
- Likewise, a bedroom door should not directly face another door or, worse still, half of another door. If it does, then use half mirrors to correct the situation.
- Make sure that you cannot see your reflection in any mirror from the bed, and especially don't have ceiling mirrors above the bed. This configuration can have serious ill-effects on your relationships.
- Make sure that no sharp wall or major furniture corners point toward the bed. This often happens with an L-shaped bedroom.
- Any open shelves should be covered or enclosed, as they act like cutting knives on the sleeper.
- Be sure not to sleep with a connecting bathroom door opening directly on to your bed. The water will drain the bedroom ch'i.
- Try not to have too many yang devices in the bedroom, such as TVs or computers.
- Don't put water features in the bedroom, as they will tend to disturb sleep, and can provoke bad luck.
- Your bed should not back on to a closed-up fireplace, as this will take much of the romance out of your relationship.
- At the family level, the general rule is that the younger members should use Easterly bedrooms while the older generation should occupy West-facing ones.

After you have taken the above into account, try to sleep with your head pointing toward your sheng ch'i or nien yen Direction. To determine your best bed orientation, you need to know your kua number (see page 31). If it's not practical to sleep with your head pointing in your best Direction, then at least try to utilize one of your other three good Directions. Don't attempt to put the bed diagonally into a corner to achieve one of these configurations, as the resultant triangular hollow deprives the headboard of support.

Above: *The headboard has plenty of support in this bedroom, but disturbing ch'i descending from the beam could trouble the sleepers' rest.*

Best bed Directions

KUA NUMBER	DIRECTION
1	S
2	NW
3	SE
4	E
5 (male)	NW
5 (female)	W
6	SW
7	NE
8	W
9	N

Bedroom — bad feng shui

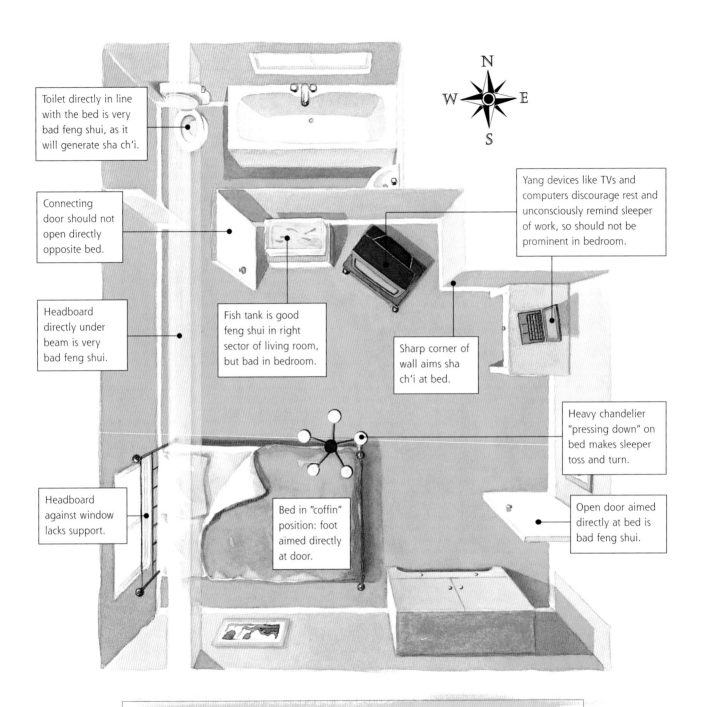

Toilet directly in line with the bed is very bad feng shui, as it will generate sha ch'i.

Connecting door should not open directly opposite bed.

Headboard directly under beam is very bad feng shui.

Fish tank is good feng shui in right sector of living room, but bad in bedroom.

Yang devices like TVs and computers discourage rest and unconsciously remind sleeper of work, so should not be prominent in bedroom.

Sharp corner of wall aims sha ch'i at bed.

Heavy chandelier "pressing down" on bed makes sleeper toss and turn.

Headboard against window lacks support.

Bed in "coffin" position: foot aimed directly at door.

Open door aimed directly at bed is bad feng shui.

In this bedroom it's a wonder the occupant gets any sleep at all. A beam and chandelier "press down" on the bed, the wall and toilet point sha ch'i at it, the bed is in the "coffin" position facing an open door, and the headboard gets no support at all from the window directly behind. Also, both the fish tank and the electronic equipment such as the TV and the computer are bad feng shui in a bedroom, the latter in particular unconsciously reminding the sleeper of work and thus discouraging rest.

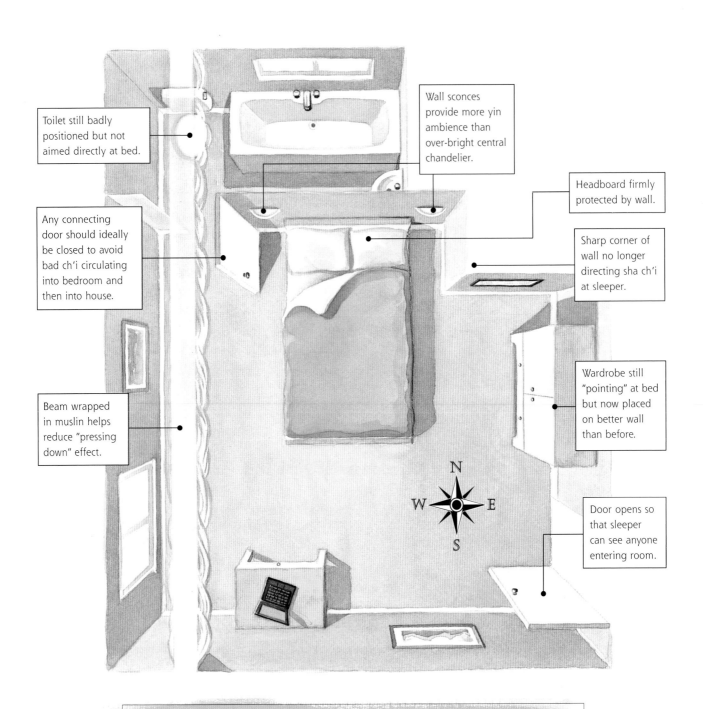

Toilet still badly positioned but not aimed directly at bed.

Wall sconces provide more yin ambience than over-bright central chandelier.

Headboard firmly protected by wall.

Any connecting door should ideally be closed to avoid bad ch'i circulating into bedroom and then into house.

Sharp corner of wall no longer directing sha ch'i at sleeper.

Beam wrapped in muslin helps reduce "pressing down" effect.

Wardrobe still "pointing" at bed but now placed on better wall than before.

Door opens so that sleeper can see anyone entering room.

N
W E
S

Although the computer is still present, the bedroom is now much more likely to be a place of peace and rest. The bed is up against a wall for support and is no longer in the "coffin" position. Nor does it have sha ch'i aimed at it, or a heavy beam "pressing down" on top of it. The beam itself has been "hidden" by a muslin wrap. Wall lights in place of the central chandelier generate a yin light, much more appropriate for a bedroom than bright, yang illumination. Wall colors are now a more passive, calming and yin blue, reducing stress and inducing sleep.

Child's bedroom

Best child's bed Directions

CHILD	DIRECTION
Eldest son	E (a strong yang position)
Middle son	N
Youngest son	NE
Eldest daughter	SE
Middle daughter	S
Youngest daughter	W

A child's bedroom is an interesting dilemma for the feng shui practitioner. On one hand, it is a place that will see lots of bright yang play. On the other hand, it needs to be sufficiently yin to lull the child to sleep at the end of the day. This dilemma can be partly resolved by painting the room in light, bright yang colors for the daytime and so arranging the curtains and lighting that a more yin atmosphere can be created in the evening. The main light source should not be above the head of the bed, although a reading light can be positioned there.

Generally, placing the child's bedroom in the Northeast, East, or Southeast part of the house is more yang and therefore more appropriate than having it in the Northwest, Southwest, or West part. Since specific Directions are associated with specific members of the family, children (with the exception of the youngest daughter—see table left) should ideally be placed on the Central or East (yang side) of the home. This, however, is a counsel of perfection and can be followed only if rooms are available for such a choice.

One of the most important functions feng shui layout can perform in a child's room is to limit the effect of nightmares. Many practitioners have found that the application of basic feng shui rules has often critically changed the child's tendency to have nightmares. In the case of young children it has even cleared up bed-wetting.

General rules

- Try to ensure that nothing presses down on the bed, such as a large lampshade, a beam, or, worst of all, overhanging shelves.
- The child's lines of sight should be unimpeded so that he/she can see the doorway and every part of the room from the bed. This is good psychology as well as good feng shui; leave no space in which monsters might lurk!
- Make sure that the headboard is firmly against a wall, so the child is well "backed." Don't be tempted to hang heavy pictures on the wall behind the bed: children are very sensitive to the implied threat that objects may fall on their head while sleeping. The foot of the bed should not point directly out of the door—the so called "coffin" position.

Computers

Although a computer is typically found in many children's bedrooms, it is really too yang for a bedroom. At night it is best turned off and covered over.

• It is very important that there be no mirror directly visible from the bed. If there is, the child might wake in the night and catch sight of a moving reflection. This is both bad feng shui and, in the half light of the night, potentially very frightening. Incidentally, never refuse a child a night-light if it makes them happier. Just make sure it is low wattage and positioned low down—for example, plugged into an outlet near the baseboard.

• Clutter is a particularly important issue for children's bedrooms. Children always create clutter, and the best any long-suffering adult can do is provide plenty of storage space, in the hope that the child will use it. From a feng shui point of view, it is important that this clutter be not stuffed under the bed, where it can trap the free flow of ch'i. Remember, real clutter is the stuff that does not move from week to week. A daily scattering of toys does not really threaten the feng shui of a room.

• If possible, align the bed so that its head faces one of the four good Directions of the child in question, just as you would in an adult bedroom.

• If the child also uses the bedroom for doing homework, place the desk in the Northeast quarter, or face the chair in that Direction, as this is the education sector. If this faces a window then crystals to diffract the Northeast light are particularly good, as Earth is the Element of the Northeast sector. Don't hang athletic trophies, scarves, and pictures of sports teams in this sector, as they might prove something of a distraction.

Above: *From a feng shui point of view, a child's bedroom should be clutter-free and the headboard should be up against the wall with no shelves, lights or other heavy objects above it.*

Below: *Being yang, electrical equipment is unsuitable for bedrooms, but in the case of teenagers may be unavoidable.*

Child's bedroom — bad feng shui

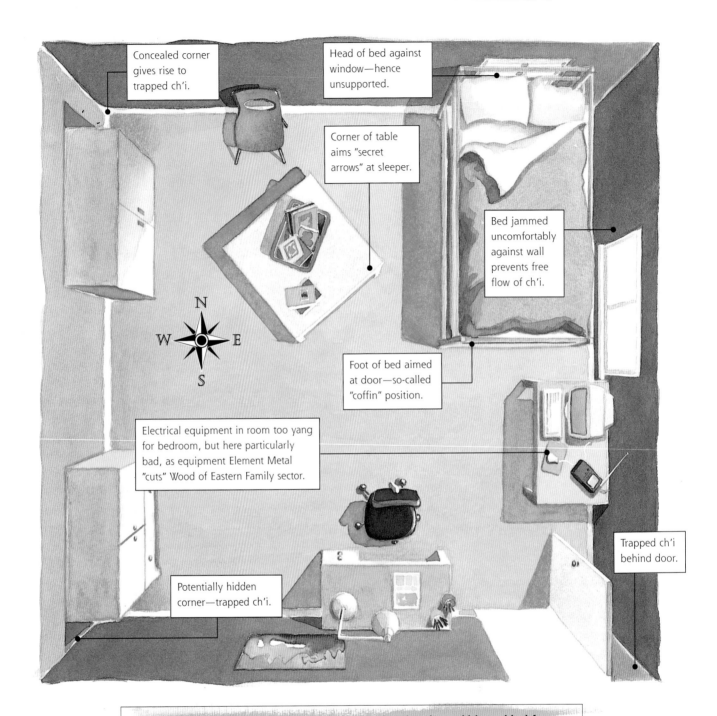

Concealed corner gives rise to trapped ch'i.

Head of bed against window—hence unsupported.

Corner of table aims "secret arrows" at sleeper.

Bed jammed uncomfortably against wall prevents free flow of ch'i.

Foot of bed aimed at door—so-called "coffin" position.

Electrical equipment in room too yang for bedroom, but here particularly bad, as equipment Element Metal "cuts" Wood of Eastern Family sector.

Trapped ch'i behind door.

Potentially hidden corner—trapped ch'i.

This child's bedroom is decorated in cool, passive yin colors, which are ideal for a sleeping area, but other features create very bad feng shui. For a start, the bed is in the "coffin" position. Also, it is jammed in a corner, so preventing the flow of ch'i, and the headboard is unsupported by the window behind. If there is a mirror in the room ensure that it is not pointing at the bed or else the child might catch sight of frightening reflections. The sharp corner of the table is sending "secret arrows" at the bed, and the desk and electrical equipment are both in the wrong sectors.

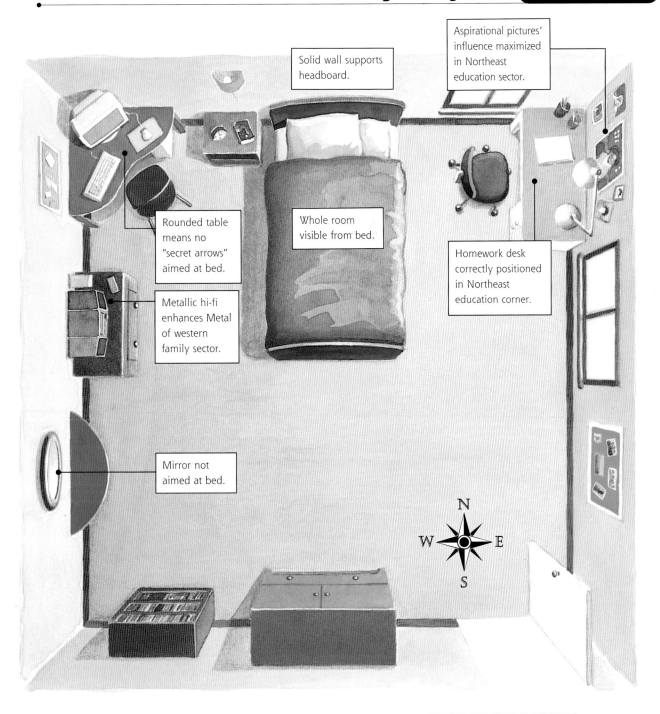

Aspirational pictures' influence maximized in Northeast education sector.

Solid wall supports headboard.

Rounded table means no "secret arrows" aimed at bed.

Whole room visible from bed.

Homework desk correctly positioned in Northeast education corner.

Metallic hi-fi enhances Metal of western family sector.

Mirror not aimed at bed.

In the rearranged bedroom (redecorated in bright, yang colors) the bunk beds— not good feng shui because the upper bunk "presses down" on the sleeper below – have been replaced by a single bed. This has been moved away from the "coffin" position and now has a wall behind it to provide support. The occupant of the bed can no longer see disturbing reflections in the mirror. The desk and Aspirational pictures are correctly positioned in the Northeast study sector, and the electrical equipment, enhances the Metal of the western children sector.

Studio apartment

Above: *In studio apartments the absence of dividing walls means that designers have greater freedom to enhance the feng shui of certain sectors.*

Elements in studios

You should try to avoid the following Elemental placements:

SECTOR	ELEMENT
N	Earth
S	Water
E	Metal
W	Fire
NE	Wood
SE	Metal
SW	Wood
NW	Fire

A studio apartment is a special case. Here the pa kua is applied simultaneously both to the whole premises and to just the one room. Clearly many of the factors relevant to non-studio apartments or houses do not apply in this situation.

The studio apartment is a world on its own. The opportunity to allocate individual rooms to the pa kua does not exist. The pa kua must be put over the whole room, dividing the area into the, by now, familiar eight sectors. Think very carefully which Aspirations you wish to promote, and hence which sectors you want to energize. You should not, especially in a small studio apartment, attempt to energize more than about three of the eight sectors. Concentrate instead on not putting conflicting Elements into any sector.

The table on the left shows the conflicting Elements for each individual sector. These conflicting Elements "destroy" the resident Element of that sector. By avoiding these, you at least avoid destroying the energy of any of the eight sectors.

As the front door often opens directly onto the main living area, thought has to be given to protecting the home from sha ch'i. Where the front door of a studio opens right into the room there is very little protection from the direct entry of unwanted energies. On the other hand, since it is an apartment, the door opens only onto a corridor, not the real "mouth" of the building (the street door), so the flow of sha ch'i is already somewhat obstructed anyway.

In traditional dwellings, a screen would be erected immediately inside the door so that anyone or anything entering would have to proceed around the screen, rather than barging straight in. In traditional Chinese thought, evil influences tended to travel in straight lines and could not manage such a maneuver. If space is limited, a screen may well be impractical, and the opportunities for controlling the ch'i flow into the apartment may be limited.

On the other hand, the fact that there are few living functions that are walled off as separate rooms gives a designer greater freedom to enhance the feng shui of certain sectors without the problems sometimes caused by walls dividing up those spaces.

Above: *Lighting can be used to highlight different sectors of a studio apartment at different times of the day.*

For example, if the Southwest or relationship sector can be decorated in Fire and Earth colors (red and yellow) and dressed with crystals and pairs of objects, then it can become a feature of the main room, rather than being limited to whatever subsidiary room happens to occupy the Southwest of a larger home.

One large studio that I remember was cleverly designed as a series of sets. Each had its own illumination, so that the dining area could be "switched on" and the bed area "switched off," or vice versa. In order to do this you need quite a large studio. In smaller studio apartments, compartmentalization can be managed with screens, or with judicious color use.

Mirrors are a major device for extending "missing corners" in feng shui. With a studio, there may be no missing corners, so mirrors have to be used carefully, or you may inadvertently extend an area, thereby diminishing another that is important to you; be very careful in your placement of large mirrors.

If your space is limited, some of your enhancements may need to be pictures of the Element rather than the Element itself. For example, to energize the Southeast prosperity sector, a large picture of moving water, like a waterfall, may need to stand in for an actual water feature such as a fountain. Pictures are obviously less effective than the real thing, although some moving light waterfall pictures (where they avoid being kitsch) can be quite effective.

DIRECTION
If you want to check in which direction a studio apartment faces, you should go by the direction of the street door of the main building, not the door of the apartment.

Studio apartment — bad feng shui

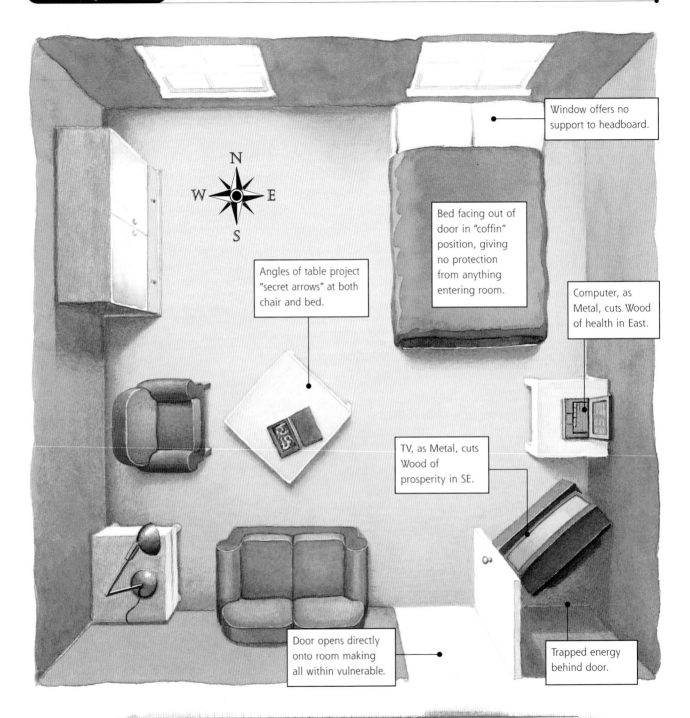

Window offers no support to headboard.

Bed facing out of door in "coffin" position, giving no protection from anything entering room.

Angles of table project "secret arrows" at both chair and bed.

Computer, as Metal, cuts Wood of health in East.

TV, as Metal, cuts Wood of prosperity in SE.

Door opens directly onto room making all within vulnerable.

Trapped energy behind door.

Something you often can't avoid in a studio is a front door opening onto the room, increasing vulnerable feelings within. In the above apartment, the situation is made worse with the bed in the so-called "coffin" position, i.e. facing directly out of the door. This, combined with the bed's unsupported head (it has a window behind it rather than a wall), deprives the sleeper of protection. Other problems are the sharp-cornered coffee table emitting "secret arrows" at the seats and computer workstation, and inappropriate Elements in the East and Southeast sectors.

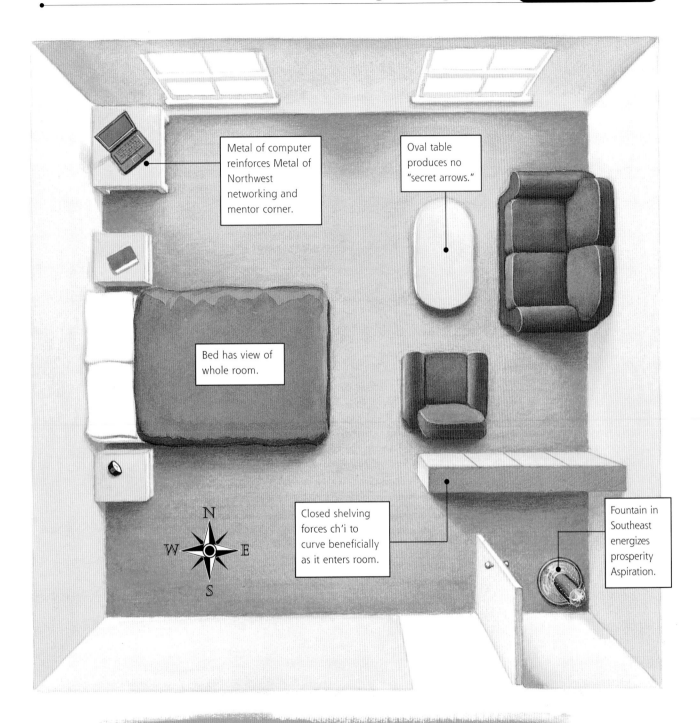

Metal of computer reinforces Metal of Northwest networking and mentor corner.

Oval table produces no "secret arrows."

Bed has view of whole room.

Closed shelving forces ch'i to curve beneficially as it enters room.

Fountain in Southeast energizes prosperity Aspiration.

Obviously the front door still opens onto the room, but the shelving unit now forces ch'i to curve beneficially as it enters the room. The bed has been re-positioned so that its headboard is supported by the wall behind and it is no longer in the "coffin" position. Other improvements are the computer in the Northwest sector (the proper sector for Metal), the fountain in the Southeast corner (where it energizes the prosperity aspiration) and the new table (no more "secret arrows").

General office

environment

The feng shui of your workplace is very important because the likelihood is that you will spend upwards of eight hours there every working day. Remember the rule: if you regularly spend time in one seat or place, it's worth checking the feng shui there. Obviously if you own the business, it is most important that you get the feng shui right in order for the business to prosper.

If you are the boss, you should improve your *own* feng shui, because the business is an extension of your decisions. Also, the feng shui of top members of staff—for example, key salesmen, the C.E.O., and the chief financial officer—should be carefully checked and changed if need be. Other less important job functions may have to take a compromize positioning. However, if the feng shui of the office overall is good, then the feng shui of individual workers will be enhanced.

THE HEAD OF THE COMPANY

If you own the business, the location of your office is very important. As a general rule, it should be as far as possible from the main entrance, but where you have an overview of as many key staff as possible (assuming it's an open-plan or semi-open-plan office). Your back should be well supported with a solid wall behind, and you should have a good view of your own office door.

Thought should be given to the positioning of your office in the overall office floor plan. Using the pa kua, you might position this office in the knowledge (Northeast) sector if it is a knowledge-based business, or in the mentor/networking sector (Northwest) if the business especially relies upon contacts with other outside businesses. A favorite, of course, is the Southwest or wealth position, but often this may be more appropriate for wealth-producing staff such as key sales people.

General rules

- Make sure that the entrance is wide and well lit with a "bright hall" area for ch'i collection in front of the main doors. Make sure that trash from neighboring businesses or homes does not accumulate in front of your door.
- Light the entranceway well with, for example, uplights.
- If the option exists, protect the entrance of your office building with two stone/cement lions (sometimes called fu dogs), such as you sometimes see outside large Chinese banks or restaurants. These help to reduce the entry into the building of bad, or sha, ch'i. Positioning of these often requires landlord and local building code permission, however, which may not be easy to obtain.
- Putting a moving water feature at or near the main door will welcome in good ch'i. A bubbling water column is useful here.
- Avoid long, straight corridor or furniture alignments.
- Make sure that the office layout is such that people (and therefore ch'i) can move smoothly through the office without bumping into badly placed furniture. Get rid of as many sharp corners as you can.

- Activate the prosperity sector in the Southeast by using Water features here, such as fountains or fish tanks with eight bright fish, plus one dark one to represent balancing yin.
- Activate the fame sector (South), especially if your business depends on public recognition, by installing red furnishings or other representatives of Fire, such as strong lighting.
- Activate the networking sector (Northwest) of your business with Metal—filing cabinets and electronic equipment will do. Alternatively, you could use Metal's producing Element, Earth, for example in the form of large crystals.
- Some practitioners recommend activating the career (North) sector of an office, but this tends to promote the careers of *all* members of staff and may therefore lead to mass departures. Ideally you should keep activation of this sector to your home. But if you do want to activate this sector in the office, use a Water feature, like an aquarium.
- More advanced feng shui takes account of the movement of specific influences or "Stars." If, for example, you have a room or office in which the Five Yellow Star happens to be located at a particular time, you should not refurbish the room until the Star has changed position. You will need a good feng shui practitioner to calculate your Flying Stars.

Above: *Guardian lions or fu dogs, either side of an office front door help to prevent the entry of bad or sha ch'i, but they are not always practical.*

Above: *Large windows leave these office workers' backs unsupported.*

General office — bad feng shui

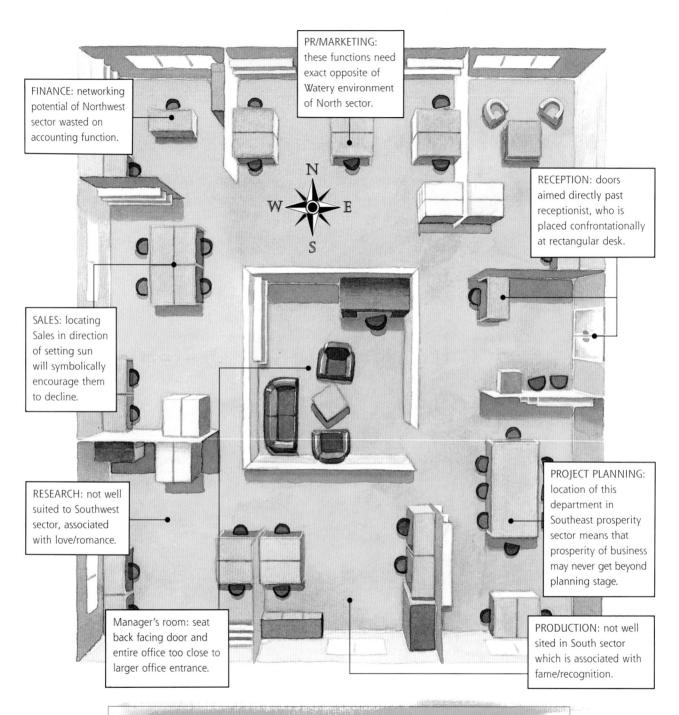

FINANCE: networking potential of Northwest sector wasted on accounting function.

PR/MARKETING: these functions need exact opposite of Watery environment of North sector.

RECEPTION: doors aimed directly past receptionist, who is placed confrontationally at rectangular desk.

SALES: locating Sales in direction of setting sun will symbolically encourage them to decline.

RESEARCH: not well suited to Southwest sector, associated with love/romance.

PROJECT PLANNING: location of this department in Southeast prosperity sector means that prosperity of business may never get beyond planning stage.

Manager's room: seat back facing door and entire office too close to larger office entrance.

PRODUCTION: not well sited in South sector which is associated with fame/recognition.

Only a quick glance is needed to see how badly this office is arranged. The center or tai ch'i, which should be open, is blocked by the manager's office. All the subordinate departments of the office, apart from reception, are in the wrong sectors. Within departments, facing desks are confrontational, rigid alignments mean beneficial ch'i moves past, and many chair backs are "unprotected," leaving their occupants vulnerable to "attack" from behind. Lots of sharp edges and narrow openings impede the free flow of ch'i.

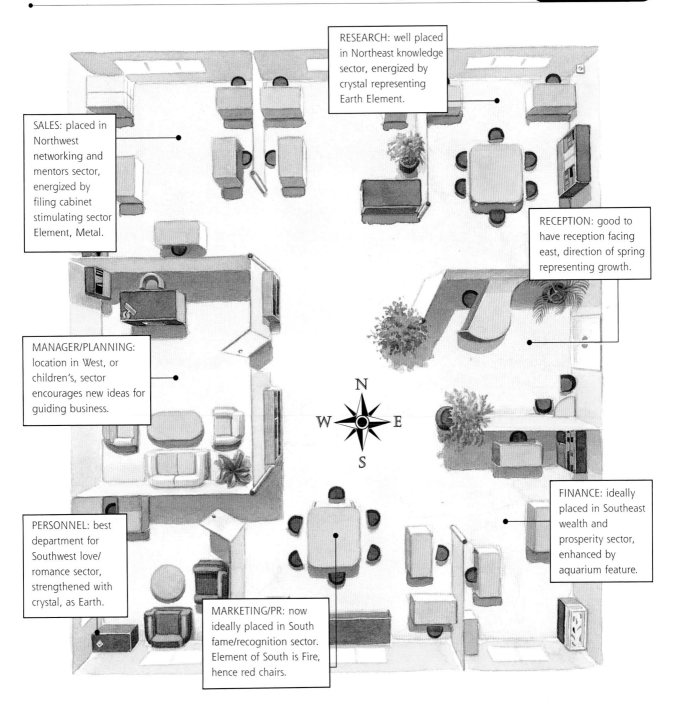

RESEARCH: well placed in Northeast knowledge sector, energized by crystal representing Earth Element.

SALES: placed in Northwest networking and mentors sector, energized by filing cabinet stimulating sector Element, Metal.

RECEPTION: good to have reception facing east, direction of spring representing growth.

MANAGER/PLANNING: location in West, or children's, sector encourages new ideas for guiding business.

PERSONNEL: best department for Southwest love/romance sector, strengthened with crystal, as Earth.

MARKETING/PR: now ideally placed in South fame/recognition sector. Element of South is Fire, hence red chairs.

FINANCE: ideally placed in Southeast wealth and prosperity sector, enhanced by aquarium feature.

The office is now much improved. Reception is more welcoming with a curved desk; the tai ch'i is open; sharp corners are softened by plants and columns on the ends of partitions; desks are no longer symbolically confrontational and most chair backs are well "supported." Shelving units are closed, so avoiding generation of harmful "secret arrows." Most importantly, the various office departments are now in the appropriate sectors, so stimulating the growth and success of the business. The walls have been repainted an energizing green color encouraging motivation in the workplace.

Your office

environment

Above: *At meetings, even small ones, make sure that you are facing your sheng ch'i, or at least one of your other three good Directions.*

In any office environment you have to accept that certain areas are outside your control. But as far as your own desk is concerned—or, if you are lucky enough to have one, your own office—you do have some autonomy. You may not be able to place your desk in the optimal position, such as diagonally to others, for example, but by exercising a little ingenuity you can still carry out an effective feng shui office makeover. First of all, follow such of the general office rules set out on pages 74—5 as apply. Then carry on as below.

General rules

- The most important consideration is to ensure that your desk is not hit by "secret arrows." In other words, avoid locating it at the end of a long corridor, or pointed at by the corners of walls, pillars or other desks. This is most important. If you are unable to get your desk moved, then try to blunt the "secret arrows" by placing softeners such as plants or screens in front of them.

- Your line of sight is also very important. It is not for nothing that the expression "commanding view" also carries the connotation of controlling. It is important to have the levers of power in front of you, not behind.

- That other great expression, "stabbed in the back," also sums up the feng shui prohibition against showing your back to an open space, a door or a corridor.

- Make sure that you are well supported. Kings and queens instinctively knew the benefits of a high-backed throne, placed in front of an impressive wall. Make sure your office chair is backed by a wall. Often chairs back on to windows—this is not a good feng shui position.

- If you introduce indoor plants into the office, make sure they are the round-leaved, fleshy variety, not sharp or spiky. Above all, make sure that they are healthy and flourishing and stay that way. You do not want them introducing too much yin into what should be a predominantly dynamic yang atmosphere.

• If you are not the owner of the business you might want to energize the North (career) sector of your personal office.

• Make sure that you can clearly see the doorway of your own office.

• Try to position yourself facing one of your four best Directions, or if possible your absolutely best Direction, your sheng ch'i. See page 30 for how to calculate this. If there is a conflict between this and considerations of "secret arrows," then the latter always take precedence.

• If you are not the master of your own space in the office, then concentrate on the micro feng shui of your desk. Eliminate surrounding clutter. Throw away those non-essential piles of paper you have been keeping just in case, or at least put them out of sight in a filing cabinet. Remember, the old saying "Out of sight, out of mind" means that they no longer act as subconscious energy drainers. Out of sight means out of mind, but, more importantly, out of the feng shui environment.

• Eliminate clutter on your desk by improving the filing system, using trays and reducing unnecessarily full intrays.

• Institute procedures to keep different projects separately in appropriately marked folders.

• Stimulate the same quarters on your desk that you might have stimulated if you had had the power to change the whole room by using inventiveness. For example, a desk lamp to the South, or the farthest edge of your desk, could improve your "fame" and help raise your profile within the organization.

Above: *Sharp and angular desks are not good feng shui. The end desk is particularly vulnerable with its back to the door. (The square pillars should be softened, perhaps with a climbing plant.) Facing desks are confrontational.*

Below: *The person who sits at this desk has no "support" for his back and cannot see his own office door.*

Your office — bad feng shui

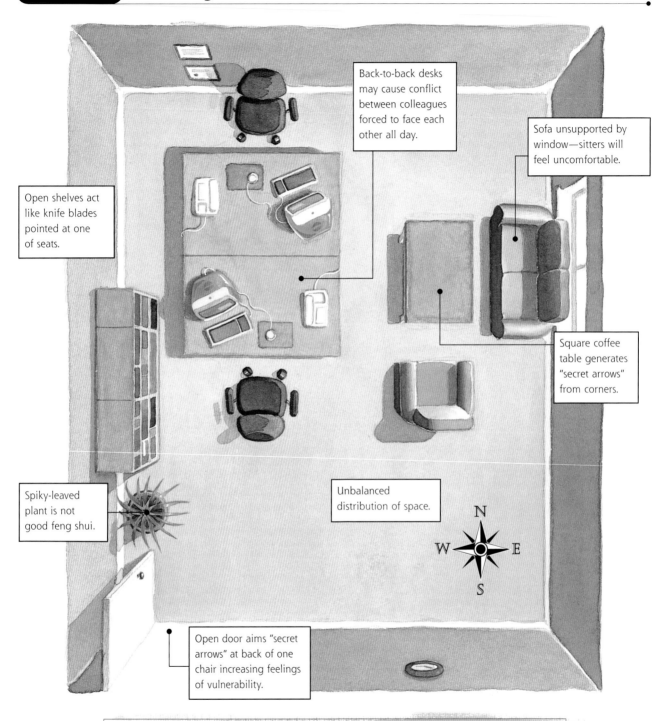

Back-to-back desks may cause conflict between colleagues forced to face each other all day.

Sofa unsupported by window—sitters will feel uncomfortable.

Open shelves act like knife blades pointed at one of seats.

Square coffee table generates "secret arrows" from corners.

Spiky-leaved plant is not good feng shui.

Unbalanced distribution of space.

Open door aims "secret arrows" at back of one chair increasing feelings of vulnerability.

This small office is badly organized in a number of ways. The two colleagues sit facing each other in a symbolically confrontational way. One also has his/her back to the door, making them vulnerable to anyone entering the room. The seating area has a sofa unsupported by a wall behind and a coffee table with sharp corners generating "secret arrows." More "secret arrows" aimed directly at one of the office's occupants come from the open shelving unit. The feng shui of the room is further degraded by the spiky-leaved plant.

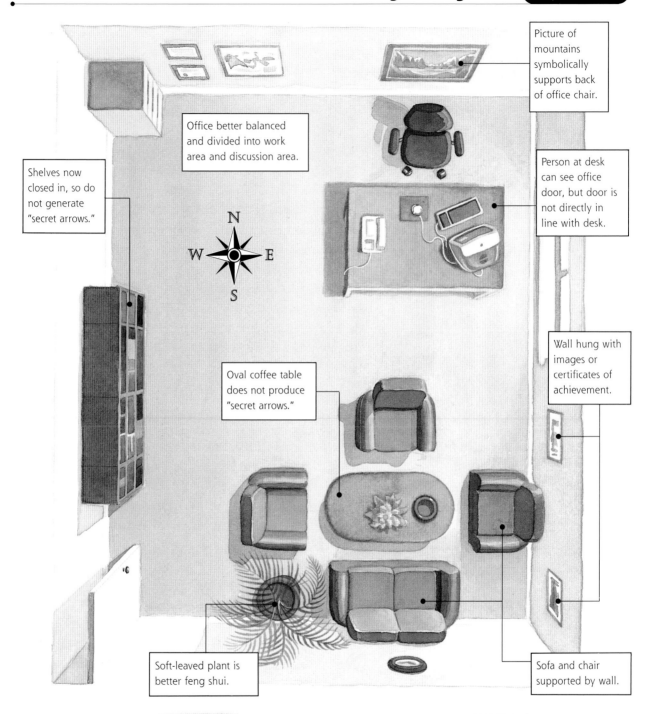

Picture of mountains symbolically supports back of office chair.

Office better balanced and divided into work area and discussion area.

Shelves now closed in, so do not generate "secret arrows."

Person at desk can see office door, but door is not directly in line with desk.

Wall hung with images or certificates of achievement.

Oval coffee table does not produce "secret arrows."

Soft-leaved plant is better feng shui.

Sofa and chair supported by wall.

One of the desks has now been removed, so the office's sole occupant has a full view of the room and door. He/she is backed by an impressive wall hung with pictures, one of which shows mountains, symbolizing support. A filing cabinet energizes the Metal of the Northwest networking sector); the shelves are closed; and the seating area has a supported sofa and an oval, corner-less coffee table emitting no unwelcome "secret arrows." The fern-like plant and the certificates of achievement on the wall further enhance the overall feng shui.

Garden

Above: *Often dismissed as bad feng shui because they are stunted, bonsai trees actually make good Wood Element energizers, especially if used indoors.*

Below: *Water features should be sited and designed with great care, as water is important in feng shui.*

In Chinese and Japanese traditions, the garden was very carefully designed to imitate natural landscapes, but in a stylish and whimsical or exaggerated way. The Imperial Palace Summer Gardens near Beijing in China came complete with their own lake and miniature mountains, which provided specially crafted views. The microcosm of the garden was meant to reflect the macrocosm of the world. The Chinese view is that the garden should be nature made perfect. The Japanese cultivate this even more extremely and in a very stylized way. Feng shui features are common in these gardens. For example, bridges will often turn at right angles in the middle of a lake or stream. This avoids creating fast-moving ch'i, which would be the result of a long, straight bridge.

Trees are often cut back in a stylish way, which finds its ultimate expression in bonsai, where miniature landscapes are created with real trees that are artificially stunted. It has sometimes been argued that bonsai is bad feng shui, because the natural growth energy has been restricted, but the careful planning that goes into these perfect miniatures belies that. Bonsai make quite good Wood Element energizers when used indoors.

Water is a key feng shui feature. The austere lines of the Zen garden went even further and often used raked swirls of gravel to symbolize real streams. Where real water was not practical, gravel acted as an imitation. This principle could be echoed in the design of a domestic Western garden today.

Of course, because water is such an important feature in feng shui, there are complex Water Dragon formulas, outside the scope of this book, which give precise directions for placing a water feature in the garden. These depend on the exact degrees of the front door or ch'i mouth of the house, and vary from period to period. Unless you make a special study of these methods, it is best to leave the siting of a significant body of water to a traditionally trained professional.

Feng shui is at the heart of traditional Chinese gardens. Not only must the gardens imitate nature, they must also improve on nature. These gardens were made not only to encourage contemplation and a feeling of stillness, related to the mental disciplines of Zen (or Chan in the Chinese tradition). They were also there to balance yin and yang and provide a feng shui setting for the house, temple, or palace.

If you are lucky enough to have your own garden, you have an excellent opportunity to practice traditional feng shui and significantly improve the feng shui of your home. In your garden there should be none of the rigid formality of French château gardens, where everything is squared off. Nor should there be the long, straight walks favored by English country houses. Instead, the lines of the garden should be curved and flow so that the ch'i energy is conducted through the garden, but contained.

Make sure that no paths cut straight through your garden and out the other side. Straight paths are anathema in a feng shui garden. This is especially true of the traditional straight path that, in Britain, is often found linking the front door directly to the front gate. If there is an opportunity to curve this without—for example, destroying an original feature like a tessellated pavement, then by all means move the gate so that it is not directly in front of the door. Often this is not a practical thing to do, for example, if the space between door and gate is very short.

Feng shui was first applied to the landscape, so the earliest rules of what is called traditional Form School feng shui govern the garden. Any site is supposed to be surrounded by the four Celestial Animals (see pages 24—5). Try to organize the garden so that the supporting Black Tortoise occurs at the back of the house. This position is where you should build a rock garden or other high supportive feature. If this protective backing, in the form of a building, a tall wall or some other structure behind the house is not present, then planting a line of tall trees here is an excellent idea.

Conversely, in front of the house there should, if possible, be an open area to allow beneficial ch'i to settle and accumulate. This is referred to as the ming tang. In general terms, if you are going to have a water feature, especially if it is a flowing one, then—using the Form School ideal model, it should be in front of this open area. Then, beyond this again, there can be a small

Above: *Paths should flow and curve to conduct ch'i through the garden.*

Above: *Paved terraces make good ming tang areas for collecting ch'i before it enters the house.*

Below: *Twists and turns and surprise vistas are at the heart of a good feng shui garden.*

hillock or a low wall. From a symbolic point of view, this is the Red Phoenix (Red Bird).

On either side of your house there should be the vegetative equivalent of enfolding hills. Remember that the right side, as you look out of the front door, is the yin White Tiger. It should be lower than the left side which is the yang Green Dragon. A hedge or other strongly growing green feature is good on that side. Remember, if the yin side is naturally more prominent, strengthen the yang Dragon side with strong garden lights to give it more prominence.

The outside is sometimes said to be governed by the Earlier Heaven Sequence of the Trigrams. For simplicity, however, and because recent books on feng shui in the garden stick to the familiar Later Heaven Sequence of the Trigrams, we will use this to suggest typical planting positions for your garden.

First sketch your garden out on a piece of paper. Overlay the familiar nine-chamber lo shu pattern (see page 26). Now use a compass to orient it in relation to your garden, and mark in the eight Directions. Referring to the guide shown opposite, add to each of these Directions their associated Elements and colors.

When choosing plants, use this chart as a color guide, so that bright fiery red flowers will tend to be planted to the South, and so on.

Above: *The raised creeper-covered boundary to the left of this garden represents the yang Green Dragon, one of the four Celestial Animals.*

This color scheme does not have to be rigidly adhered to, as some books suggest, but is simply symbolically suggestive. Of greater importance is the observation of the Elements when placing garden furniture.

If putting in a metal swing, choose the Northwest or West side to coincide with the Element of Metal. A barbecue should ideally go in the South, although this may not always be practical. Feng shui is, to a large extent, all about compromize—energizing those areas important to you. Using this rule it is tempting to say that water features should go on the North side of the garden, but remember that water in feng shui is a special case, and its positioning needs to be planned carefully.

Try to plant shrubs and trees in such a way that the visitor to the garden cannot see everything at once. He or she should be surprised by new vistas at each turning. There should be, if space permits, secret bowers and hidden views. Mix yin and yang, shade and sun, in interesting combinations—don't allow either shade or sun to predominate. Any good gardener will recognize the benefits of this immediately.

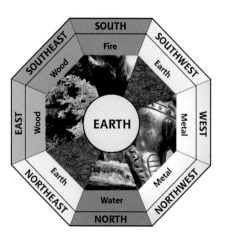

Above: *Use this Direction, Element, and color guide when planning your garden.*

Front garden — bad feng shui

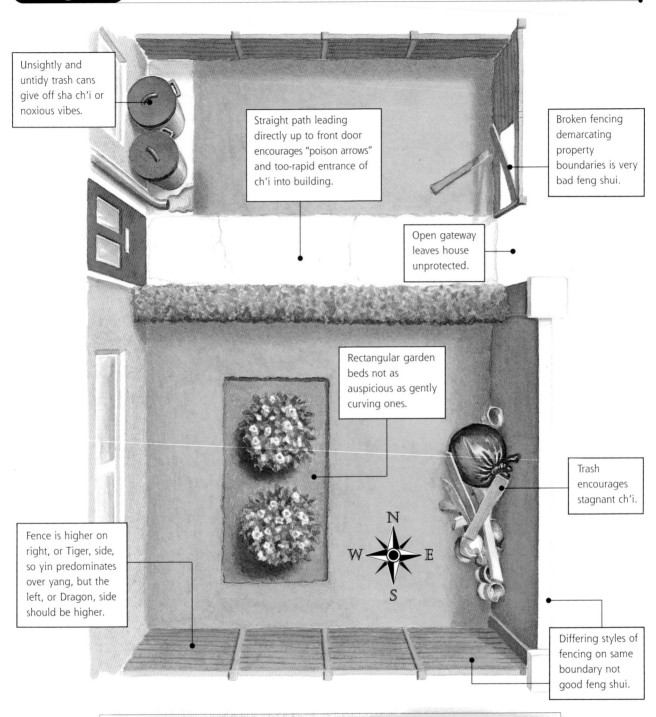

Unsightly and untidy trash cans give off sha ch'i or noxious vibes.

Straight path leading directly up to front door encourages "poison arrows" and too-rapid entrance of ch'i into building.

Broken fencing demarcating property boundaries is very bad feng shui.

Open gateway leaves house unprotected.

Rectangular garden beds not as auspicious as gently curving ones.

Trash encourages stagnant ch'i.

Fence is higher on right, or Tiger, side, so yin predominates over yang, but the left, or Dragon, side should be higher.

Differing styles of fencing on same boundary not good feng shui.

Everything is wrong with this front yard. The absence of a gate leaves the house unprotected. The straight path encourages "poison arrows" and allows ch'i to rush toward the house too fast. Trash cans and debris generate sha and stagnant ch'i. The flower bed is too sharp and square, and the right-hand, or Tiger, side garden fence is higher than the left-hand, or Dragon, side. This means that yin dominates over yang: in a home it should be the other way around.

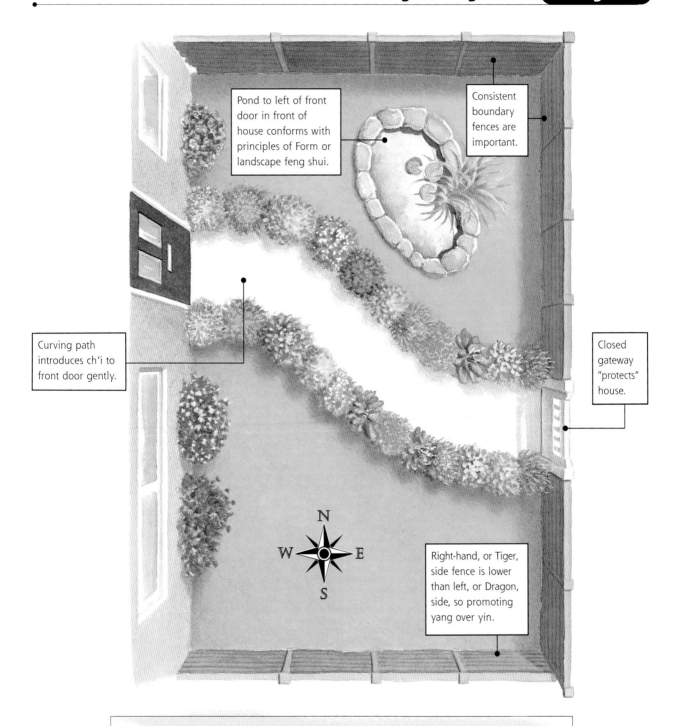

Pond to left of front door in front of house conforms with principles of Form or landscape feng shui.

Consistent boundary fences are important.

Curving path introduces ch'i to front door gently.

Closed gateway "protects" house.

Right-hand, or Tiger, side fence is lower than left, or Dragon, side, so promoting yang over yin.

Following a feng shui makeover, the front yard is much improved. A new gate protects the house and a curving path both avoids "poison arrows" and slows down beneficial ch'i as it approaches the house. All trash has been removed, as has the rectangular and inauspicious flower bed. The fence on the right-hand side has been lowered so that yang now correctly predominates over yin. A new feature is the pond, which enhances the overall flow of the garden, as established by the sinuous front path.

Back garden — bad feng shui

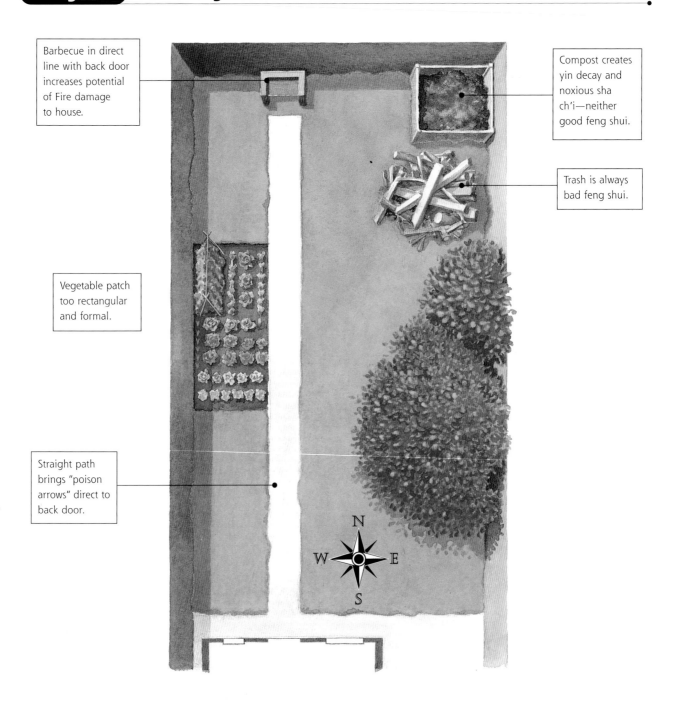

Barbecue in direct line with back door increases potential of Fire damage to house.

Compost creates yin decay and noxious sha ch'i—neither good feng shui.

Trash is always bad feng shui.

Vegetable patch too rectangular and formal.

Straight path brings "poison arrows" direct to back door.

The back garden suffers from some of the same faults as the original front garden, notably the straight path, the rectangular cultivated bed, and the presence of trash. But in addition, the barbecue faces the back door, thus increasing the potential for fire damage to the house. The presence of the compost pile creates decay, which is yin, and also noxious sha ch'i, both of which are bad feng shui.

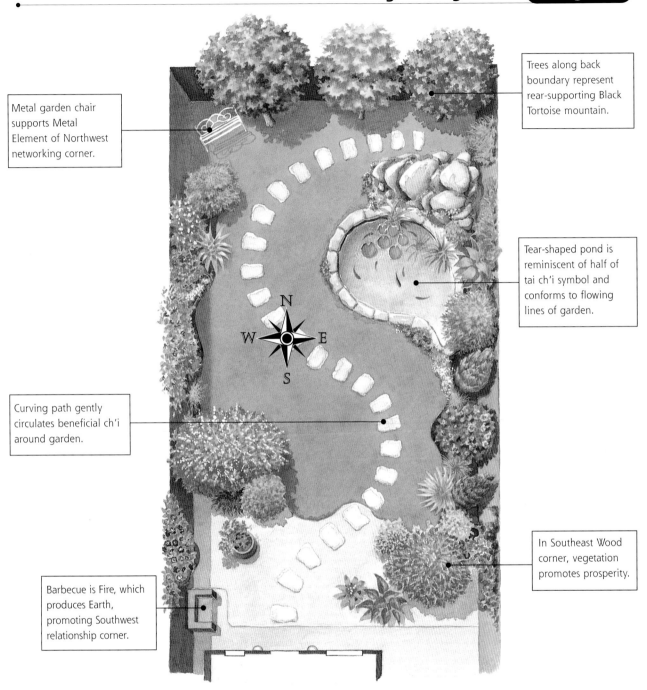

Metal garden chair supports Metal Element of Northwest networking corner.

Trees along back boundary represent rear-supporting Black Tortoise mountain.

Tear-shaped pond is reminiscent of half of tai ch'i symbol and conforms to flowing lines of garden.

Curving path gently circulates beneficial ch'i around garden.

Barbecue is Fire, which produces Earth, promoting Southwest relationship corner.

In Southeast Wood corner, vegetation promotes prosperity.

The curving path now conducts beneficial ch'i in the correct manner. The line of trees along the back boundary and the rock garden behind the pond support the rear of the house by symbolizing the Black Tortoise mountain. The barbecue is repositioned in the Southwest corner, where, as Fire, it produces Earth, beneficial in this relationship sector. Opposite, new planting in the Southeast corner promotes the prosperity of the household. Finally, in the Northwest corner, a metal garden bench supports the Metal Element of the Northwest sector, associated with networking and mentors.

Case studies

Above: *Large cactus plants have no place in feng shui-regulated homes. They can be especially damaging when placed in the relationship/romance corner.*

Below: *Earth, Fire, and crystal can be used to energize the Earth (Southwest) sector.*

JANE AND DORIAN

Jane and Dorian were on the point of breaking up after a long and fruitful relationship. For some reason, Jane could no longer stand all those little habits that she used to find so endearing in Dorian. Dorian, for his part, couldn't remember what he had ever seen in Jane, although he still found her very attractive sexually.

Jane was thinking over what had happened to them, when it occurred to her that friends had given them a large cactus for their recent anniversary, and that she had put it in the Southwest corner of their living room. Suddenly, something she remembered reading about feng shui came to mind.

Spiky cactus

When she looked it up, Jane found that the Southwest was indeed the relationship corner; and she had placed this large, irritable-looking cactus right there in pride of place. Worse than that, Jane learned that cactus, being a growing plant, was Wood and that Wood destroyed Earth, which was the Element of the Southwest. She was destroying the Element of the romance corner. How could she have been so stupid? Here's how Jane repaired the damage:

- She gave the cactus away. Such a spiky, irritable plant has no place in a feng shui-regulated home.
- She checked that the predominant color in the Southwest was yellow (Earth). Adding highlights of red (the color of Fire) to this corner helped to stimulate Earth by introducing its producing Element, Fire.
- Finding a rock to place in this corner was more difficult, but Jane finally settled for a large amethyst crystal.
- To further stimulate Fire here, she added a pair of red candles. By using a pair she added to the symbolism of a couple. Had they been available, a pair of mandarin ducks (famous for their lifelong loyalty) would have added to the symbolic feng shui.
- A photo of herself and Dorian at the height of their relationship completed the picture. Later that evening, over a candlelit dinner, they patched up their most recent differences. Neither is quite sure when it happened, but later that week they both admitted that they didn't find each other as irritating as before. The relationship survived, and the couple are still together.

JAMES AND SARAH

James and his wife, Sarah, moved into a basement apartment. Soon after, James lost his job, one of their daughters developed sleeping problems, and Sarah started quarreling with her parents. Any house move is a strain, but in this case bad feng shui was added to the stress of relocation.

A consultant called in to diagnose the problem put the following changes in hand. First, the apartment was cleared of all clutter and a space-clearing ceremony performed. Although not part of traditional feng shui, space-clearing provides a good base for subsequent feng shui corrections.

The gloomy entrance to the apartment was painted bright yang colors, mainly yellow because the entrance faced an Earth direction. External lights were further provided to encourage the entrance of sheng ch'i into what previously had been a very yin and discouraging entrance.

Their child was moved to a better-ventilated room and put into an ordinary bed rather than the new bunk bed which noticeably "pressed down" upon her as she slept. She was also given a nightlight. James' bedhead direction was pointing in his "total loss" Direction. This was changed so that the couple slept with James' head pointing in his third best Direction. This also happened to be Sarah's best Direction—in other words her sheng ch'i.

Above: *Bunk beds tend not to be good feng shui because the upper bunk "presses down" on the sleeper in the lower bunk.*

Aquarium

To improve Sarah's relationship with her family, the Family Direction (East) was enhanced with a vigorous indoor plant, reinforcing the Wood Element of this Direction. The career corner of the living room had an aquarium installed, with the intention of procuring James a new job. Lastly, the apartment was checked for geopathic stress and appropriate rectifications put in place.

Within two weeks the energy had begun to flow more correctly and all of the above difficulties were reversed, with the exception of James' job. Instead, Sarah landed a job that paid much better than James' old job. The couple expressed themselves well pleased with the effect of their feng shui makeover.

Above: *Laura's best Directions are shown in warm yang colors, while her worst Directions are shown in cold yin colors. Her sheng chi, or very best, Direction is Northwest.*

Below: *The essence of feng shui is the balance of yin and yang—at its most primitive—light and shade. If you have a balcony, try to make sure that it gets both in roughly equal measure.*

LAURA

When Laura moved into her new apartment she decided to carry out a complete feng shui makeover. The function of each room was already determined: there were two bedrooms and a living room-dining room, plus a kitchen, bathroom, closet, and balcony.

When Laura's kua number was checked, it was found to be a seven. This meant she was a West Life person—someone whose best four Directions are Northwest, West, Southwest and Northeast. Looking at the two bedrooms it was soon obvious that to put Laura's bed with the head pointing in one of her good Directions was impossible in the larger of the two rooms. In the smaller, however, she was able to place her bed with the head pointing West, with a good, but not direct, view of the door. Having selected this room as her bedroom, Laura chose cool yin colors in which to decorate it.

Indoor fountain

The other bedroom she designated as her study, locating her desk and computer in the Southeast or prosperity Location and angling the chair so that she faced Northwest, her sheng ch'i or best Direction. Remembering that Water strengthens Wood, the Element of the Southeast, she further enhanced this sector with a small indoor fountain. For decoration she used bright, positive, yang colors.

Moving on to the living-dining room, she located the Southwest of the room and promptly set about energizing her romance sector. To do this, she used red candles and a pair of mandarin ducks—celebrated for their constancy. Red or Fire generates Earth, the Element of this sector.

Career sector

The bathroom was a problem as it was located in the North or career sector of her apartment. Laura solved the problem by covering the outer door with a mirror, so nullifying the influence of loss of water or ch'i. A spring catch on the door kept the door closed.

The balcony gave her the opportunity to do a little outdoor feng shui, and the judicious location of potted plants in the Southeast (prosperity) and South (fame) sectors helped complete the picture. A small pa kua mirror on the outer edge of the balcony helped to defeat the oppressive effect of a large apartment block opposite. Remembering that the pa kua mirror is designed to reflect back the "poison arrows" bringing bad ch'i, she placed it carefully, so as not to cause feng shui problems for her neighbors.

Laura's feng shui makeover was a complete success and enhanced her life in many ways.

JOHN

John was a businessman with a successful career as a high-flying executive. After joining a new company as Commercial Manager at a salary considerably above his previous one, he and his live-in girlfriend celebrated by moving to a larger apartment, and discussing the possibility of marriage.

Things went well at work, although John found himself in a rather cramped office with little in the way of facilities. Contracts were exchanged on his new apartment and he moved in over a weekend. His girlfriend jokingly suggested they check the feng shui first. John felt that things were on the up-and-up and that this precaution was not necessary.

What John did not realize was that he was moving from a flat whose front door faced his sheng ch'i, or best Direction, into one where the front door faced his lui sha, or six killings Direction. (Of course, these words don't literally mean six killings, but six forms of bad luck).

The first thing that happened was that John found himself becoming irrationally irritated with the workers under him, accusing them of laziness where before he would have smiled at their idiosyncrasies. His girlfriend noticed the same attitude beginning to pervade his home environment. Three weeks later he damaged his company car. It wasn't serious, but it was bad enough for him not to want to tell his employer.

Above: *Make sure your front door faces in one of your good Directions; otherwise, like John, you may be dogged by inexplicable bad luck.*

Resignation

When things began to sour with his girlfriend, he took her on a long weekend trip, but even then he had his luggage stolen. He got back to work late and compounded his fault by justifying it too much to his boss. A month later, while attending a perfectly ordinary meeting, he found himself telling his boss what he really thought of him and, in the heat of the moment, resigning from the job he had just started.

It did not take long before his girlfriend decided to move on, leaving John with more than a handful of lost opportunities. He realized this when he moved out of what had been, for him, an ill-fated apartment. When he chose his next apartment, he heeded his ex-girlfriend's words and checked the feng shui first. The new apartment just happened to face his second-best Direction. Even though it was smaller than the first, John decided to take it. Soon afterwards, he got a good new job and found a new girlfriend; within a year he was married and starting a family. John can't explain why his life disintegrated and then picked up again so dramatically but reckons that feng shui certainly helped.

Glossary

cardinal points North, South, East, West

chen The health Trigram, whose Direction is East

ch'i Literally "cosmic breath," it is the invisible, but vital, energy of the universe

ch'ien The heaven Trigram, whose direction is Northwest

chueh ming The Direction that represents bad luck for a person and for his or her family

compass school The Fukien school of feng shui that uses the feng shui compass to diagnose ch'i flows

Direction The way a person orients him- or herself to maximize the flow of good ch'i in his or her life; everyone has four auspicious Directions and four inauspicious Directions

Earlier Heaven Sequence The oldest layout of Trigrams, arranged in a circle such that the Trigram "ch'ien" is in the South; it is used on defensive pa kua, and for burial site feng shui

Elements The five Chinese Elements, comprising Water, Fire, Wood, Earth, and Metal

feng Literally "wind"

feng sha A bad wind that destroys ch'i

feng shui Literally "wind and water;" it is the Chinese system of maximizing the accumulation of ch'i to improve the quality of a person's life

Flying Star feng shui Using the lo shu square, good and bad time dimension feng shui for buildings can be determined

Form School Feng shui that concentrates on the landscape to determine the location of the ch'i flow

fu wei A Direction with good overall harmony

ho hai The first of a person's four bad Directions; it is the Direction of mild bad luck and minor mishaps

k'an The career Trigram whose Direction is North

ken The education Trigram whose Direction is Northeast

kua Literally "Trigram;" one of the eight sides of the pa kua

k'un The marriage Trigram whose Direction is Southwest

Later Heaven Sequence The second arrangement of the eight Trigrams, used to map the internal feng shui layout of the home or office

li The Trigram of recognition and fame, whose Direction is South

lo p'an The feng shui compass

lo shu The magic square; it consists of nine numbers that add up to 15, whatever the direction in which they are added up

lui sha A person's most unlucky Direction; it represents grievous harm to both the person who is orientated in that Direction and his or her family

ming tang Open area at the front of a building for the collection of ch'i

nien yen The Direction that will improve family relationships and ensure fertility

pa kua The eight-sided, or circular arrangement, of the eight Trigrams

"secret arrow" (also known as "poison arrow)" Invisible shaft of bad ch'i emitted by sharp or hostile objects and alignments

sha / sha ch'i Stagnant, or bad, ch'i

sheng ch'i A person's best Direction—the one that will bring most good fortune

shui Literally "water"

sun The wealth Trigram, whose Direction is Southeast

tai ch'i symbol The symbol looks like two interlocking tadpoles, one black (yang) and one white (yin)

t'ien Literally "heaven"

t'ien yi The Direction of health; facing in this Direction will also help family members who are ill

Trigram Eight figures made up of three yin (broken) or yang (unbroken) lines

tui The Trigram of children, whose Direction is West

wu kwei Literally "five ghosts" as it invokes the sudden disruption of seeing a ghost; it is the Direction that promotes sudden bad luck, such as burglary, fires, or being dismissed from a job

yang Symbolized by an unbroken line, it is male active energy, the opposite of yin

yin Symbolized by a broken line, it is female passive energy, the opposite of yang

Further Reading

There are now over 300 titles in print on feng shui, so any bibliography could quickly become a daunting list. Here I have simply selected some of the books that have acted as sources for many other authors. The most prolific feng shui author is Lillian Too. She has well over 25 books in print and, not surprisingly, covers most aspects of this fascinating subject.

BOOKS PRIMARILY ON FENG SHUI AND INTERIOR DECORATION:
Rossbach, Sarah. *Feng Shui*. Penguin, London, 1983
Rossbach, Sarah. *Interior Design with Feng-shui*. Rider, London, 1987
Skinner, Stephen. *Feng Shui for Modern Living*. Cima Books, London, 2000
EASILY ACCESSIBLE BOOKS ON FENG SHUI:
Dy, Victor. *Feng Shui for Everybody*. Renaissance, Manila, 1993
Jay, Roni. *Feng Shui in Your Garden*. Tuttle Publishing, Boston, 1998
Kwok, Man-Ho. *The Feng Shui Kit*. Tuttle Publishing, Boston, 1995
Skinner, Stephen. *Feng Shui: the Traditional Oriental Way to Enhance Your Life*. Parragon, Bristol, 1997
Too, Lillian. *Complete Illustrated Book of Feng Shui*. Sterling, New York, 1996

Too, Lillian. *Easy-to-use Feng Shui: 168 Ways to Success*. Sterling, New York, 1999
Xing, Wu. *The Feng Shui Workbook*. Tuttle Publishing, Boston, 1998
MORE TECHNICAL CLASSICS OF FENG SHUI:
Skinner, Stephen. *Living Earth Manual of Feng Shui*. Penguin, London, 1989
Too, Lillian. *Applied Pa-Kua and Lo Shu Feng Shui*. Konsep Lagenda, Kuala Lumpur, 1993
Too, Lillian. *Flying Star Feng Shui*. Konsep Lagenda, Kuala Lumpur, 2000
Walters, Derek. *Feng Shui Handbook*. Thorsons, London, 1991
Walters, Derek. *Feng Shui: Perfect Placing*. Pagoda, London, 1988
Wong, Eva. *Feng-Shui: the Ancient Wisdom*. Shambhala, Boston, 1996

Useful Contacts

WORLDWIDE
Feng Shui for Modern Living Magazine
Centennial Publishing Plc,
2nd Floor, 1–5 Clerkenwell Road,
London EC1M 5PA, UK
Tel: + 44(0)20 7251 0777
Fax: + 44(0)20 7251 5490
info@fengshui-magazine.com
www.fengshui-magazine.com

AUSTRALIA
Feng Shui Design Centre
PO Box 7788, Bondi Beach,
Sydney 2026
Tel: + 61 2 9365 7877
Fax: + 61 2 9365 7847
fengshui@real.com.au
www.real.net.au/ ~ fengshui

Feng Shui Society of Australia
PO Box 4816, Mulgraze,
Victoria 3170
Tel: + 61 3 9517 8960

AUSTRIA
Dragon & Phoenix
Kernstockgrasse 21, A–8020 Graz
Tel: + 43 31671 988898
Fax: + 43 31671 988899
office@fengshui.at
www.fengshui.at

European School of Feng Shui
Hormayrstrasse 4–8,
A–4971 Aurolmunster
Tel/Fax: + 43 512 589732
veronika@europeanfengshui.com
www.europeanfengshui.com

FRANCE
Feng Shui France
40 Avenue Guy de Maupassant,
78400 Chatou
Tel: + 33 1 3480 9030

Fax: + 33 1 3071 5020
eve.purdew@wanadoo.fr

GERMANY
Feng Shui Concepts
Bruckmannring 28,
D–85764 Oberschleissheim
Tel/Fax: + 49 89 315 5018
billretsch/@bluewim.ch
www.cuenet.ch/fengshui

International Forum: Feng Shui e.V.
Lothar B. Baier, Am Wapelsberg 32,
D–51469 Bergisch Gladbach
Tel/fax: + 49 2202 249995
info@iffs.net
www.iffs.net

HONG KONG
Feng Shui Lo (Raymond Lo)
Room 729, Star House,
Tsimshatsui, Kowloon
Tel: + 852 9082 6837
Fax: + 852 2778 5017
raymond@raymond-lo.com
www.raymond-lo.com

MALAYSIA
Yap Chen Hai Feng Shui
Center of Excellence
17–3 Jalan Hujan Rahmat 2,
Taman Overseas Union,
58200 Kuala Lumpur
Tel: + 603 7782 5363
Fax: + 603 7782 5292
fsce@ychfengshui.com
www.ychfengshui.com

U.K.
The Feng Shui Catalogue
Green Dragon House, 16
Goldsmith Road, London W3 6PX
Tel/Fax: + 44 (0)20 8992 6607
thefengshuicatalogue@virgin.net
www.thefengshuicatalogue.co.uk

Feng Shui Society
377 Edgware Road,
London W2 1BT
Tel: + 44 (0)7050 289200
Fax: + 44 (0)20 8566 0898
enquiries@fengshuisociety.org.uk
www.fengshuisociety.org.uk

The Geomancer and Feng Shui Store
PO Box 250, Woking,
Surrey GU21 1YJ
Tel: + 44 (0)7000 888989
Fax: + 44 (0)1483 488998
geomancer@dragonmagic.com
www.dragonmagic.com

The Imperial School of Feng Shui and Chinese Horoscopes
Roscrea, 60 Edinburgh Road,
Bathgate, West Lothian
Tel/Fax: + 44 (0)1506 634257
maria@isfsch.freeserve.co.uk
www.isfsch.co.uk

International School of Feng Shui
2 Cherry Orchard, Shipston on
Stour, Warwickshire CV36 4QR
Tel: + 44 (0)1608 664998
Fax: + 44 (0)1608 664997
info@fengshui-school.co.uk
www.fengshui-school.co.uk

London School of Feng Shui
70a Gladsmuir Road,
London N19 3JU
Tel: + 44 (0)20 7419 9021
Fax: + 44 (0)20 7686 2757
info@fengsuzie.com
www.fengsuzie.com

U.S.A.
Feng Shui Chicago Center Inc
3745 W Montrose,
Chicago, Ill 60618
Tel: + 1 773 478 8878

Fax: + 1 773 478 2179
fengshui@megsinet.net
www.fengshuichicagocenter.com

Feng Shui Warehouse
PO Box 6689,
San Diego, CA 92166
Tel: + 1 619 523 2158
Fax: + 1 619 523 2165
fengshuiWH@aol.com
www.fengshuiwarehouse.com

International Feng Shui Research Center
1340 Marshall Street,
Boulder, CO 80302
Tel: + 1 303 939 0033
Fax: + 1 303 939 0044
fengshui@fengshui2000.com
www.fengshui2000.com

Lin Yun Temple
2959 Russell Street,
Berkeley, CA 94705
Tel: + 1 510 841 2347
Fax: + 1 510 548 2621

Nancy Pond Smith
17878 N. Bay Road, Suite 601,
N. Miami Beach, FL 33160
Tel: + 1 305 935 9393
Fax: + 1 305 935 9394
fengshuiliving@hotmail.com
www.fengshuiliving.com

Nancy San Pietro & Associates
1684 80th Street,
Brooklyn, NY 11214
Tel: + 1 718 256 2640
Fax: + 1 718 232 8054

Index

Page references in italics are for captions